MEETING HOUSE

TO CAMP MEETING

MEETING HOUSE

TO CAMP MEETING

TOWARD A HISTORY
OF AMERICAN FREE CHURCH WORSHIP
FROM 1620 TO 1835

DOUG ADAMS

Saratoga, Modern Liturgy-Resourse Publications, 1981
and
Austin, The Sharing Company, 1981

The cover illustration (from the author's personal collection) is "Office Hunters for the Year 1834," lithograph, published by Imbert, 1834. See pages 123-125 for this imagery's relationship to the early American worship and preaching.

Our appreciation to the following publishers for permission to reprint materials within: "Free Church Worship In America From 1620 To 1835," Worship, c. Order of Saint Benedict, Collegeville, Minnesota and the North American Academy of Liturgy; and "Changing Biblical Imagery and American Identity In Seventeenth and Eighteenth Century Sermons and Arts," Papers for the Annual Meeting of the American Academy of Homiletics, c. American Academy of Homiletics.

For Harland Hogue,   Anne Scott, and   John von Rohr

"Doug Adams has done pioneering work on worship in
the free church tradition in the United States.
In an area where we believed there was little
liturgical significance, or interpreted it through
the late revivals of the early nineteenth century,
Adams has instead reconstructed and brought to our
attention the contours of rich worship traditions.
He has also, by contrast, shown that nineteenth
century revivals, allegedly built on lay involvement, in fact made the preacher more central in
worship than in the earlier period. The book is
full of surprises."

                    -- Professor John Dillenberger,
                        President, Hartford Seminary

CONTENTS

The origins of American free church worship are
unknown to nearly all Protestant and Catholic clergy
as well as laity. In the absence of such knowledge,
many American Protestants are bound to a pulpit dominated
pattern of worship which is thought to be traditional but
which dates back no further than the nineteenth century
when the scope of worship and preaching was at its nar-
rowest in terms of little personal lay participation,
minimal preaching on major social issues, and infrequent
communion. The irony is that most free church worship
is defined by nineteenth century forms when free church
worship was least free. And as a consequence in ecumenical discussions, uninformed Protestants fail to contri-
bute insights from historic patterns that would encourage
Protestants toward more frequent communion and Catholics
and Protestants toward wider personal involvement of
laity and discussion of social issues in liturgy.

Colleagues in the North American Academy of Liturgy
have convinced me that this preliminary volume is needed
to inform others of contours around which their specialized studies may take shape. This volume is not the definitive book on the history of American free church worship. That book must await discoveries from dozens of
needed future dissertations and monographs. But I hope
this volume will prompt some of those needed studies and
aid others by revealing questions and contours raised
from my research over the past decade. And for the time
being, this volume will be a useful introduction to origins of American free church worship.

To do dissertations and books on American preaching
has been easier than to do such work on worship; for the
former studies have taken volumes of sermons as their
sources which make a manageable project but distort the

resulting picture of American religion by overemphasizing
the significance and authority of ministers and the role
of those denominations whose ministers published books of
sermons.[1] Studies of worship promise to correct such
distortions in the field of American religions and to
suggest alternatives to the ministerially dominated and
narrowed patterns of worship in contemporary churches.
To do dissertations and books on fixed liturgical forms
and denominationally approved directories of worship
has been easier than to do studies of free church forms
whose descriptions are more scattered; but we need such
free church studies to know the ways a majority of Christians actually were informed in American worship through
the seventeenth and eighteenth centuries. Some excellent
studies inform us of ministers' sacramental theologies
without informing us of how they actually worshipped.[2]
So, this volume and future studies need not recapitulate
such theological discussions but rather concentrate on
worship practices.

Church records and ministers' and lay church members'
diaries and memoirs are rich sources for those who accept
the challenge to write histories of American free church
worship. In the focus of this volume, free church worship is understood as worship among Puritans, Separatists,
Baptists, and Quakers in the seventeenth and eighteenth
centuries,some Methodists in the late eighteenth century,
and Disciples of Christ in the early nineteenth century.
Although a few clergy in Presbyterian and Dutch Reformed
churches developed worship patterns bearing a resemblance
to the dominant patterns studied in this book, those two
denominations more generally followed patterns from their
established European state churches; and so, they fall
beyond the free church focus of this book.[3] Although
the time frame of this study extends from 1620 until
1835, I am interested primarily in the origins of the
patterns; and so, much of this study is devoted to the
early years.

I thank fellows of the North American Academy of

Liturgy to whom the introduction of this book was presented at the 1981 annual meeting. I especially thank Harland Hogue and James White who offered valuable insights that improved this manuscript over the past few years. I am grateful for the encouragement from Graduate Theological Union colleagues of the Area VII doctoral program in liturgy: James Empereur, Robert Mitchell, William Cieslak, and Michael Aune. Thanks are also due to members of the American Academy of Homiletics for whose 1982 annual meeting I presented the core of chapter five. I thank both academies for permision to reprint those presentations that first appeared in the North American Academy of Liturgy's Worship and the American Academy of Homiletic's volume for the 1982 annual meeting in Atlanta.[4]

Finally, I hope this volume will repay numerous masters and doctoral students with whom I have had the privilege to work these past years at Pacific School of Religion and the Graduate Theological Union. Their questions have spurred my own research; and I trust this volume raises questions in their minds to stimulate intriguing lifetimes of research. I thank Alexander Blair who extensively explored a hypothesis I framed in one course; and, as a result, we co-authored an article on which chapter five is based. And I thank Mark Sydow whose interest in seventeenth and eighteenth century worship encourages my own interest when many others around us seem interested only in the nineteenth and twentieth centuries. I trust this volume reveals how much work remains to be done in seventeenth and eighteenth century American religions and how such work is highly significant for those shaping twentieth century American religions.

                                        Doug Adams

Pacific School of Religion
Berkeley, California
August, 1981

INTRODUCTION

From the landing of the Mayflower through the American Revolution, the majority of free church clergy probably spent more time interacting with worshippers around the communion table than they did preaching from pulpits. Worship patterns varied by denomination and region; but frequent communion and substantive lay contributions to the preaching and praying characterized much free church worship in seventeenth and eighteenth century America. The original pattern emerged as follows: at the communion table, close to the worshipping congregation, the clergy often presided with lay leaders. Standing there with the people, clergy began the service with prayers of thanksgiving and later led prayers of intercession incorporating concerns spoken out or written by laity. All continued to stand for singing led by laity. Often from the table, clergy read the scriptures intersperced with exegesis so that the word would be heard and not be a dumb reading. Then they went into the pulpit to give their sermons bearing the Bible on any of a wide range of issues related to God's kingdom on earth. Immediately after the sermon as the worship continued, they came down from the pulpit and sat at the table to answer the congregation's questions and hear witnessing by laity, who were free to agree or disagree with what clergy had said. And from the table, clergy gave thanks and gave the bread and wine, as often as each Sunday or at least once a month, to lay leaders who distributed communion to the people. After more singing, the people often gave their offerings at the table. (And in afternoon worship, clergy and lay leaders led the time of censures and confessions when lay people often spoke out extensively in examinations of those presented for baptism, church membership, admonition, or excommunication.) This study specifies 1620 as

a beginning; because the Separatist community landing
at Plymouth carried with them many of these worship forms
that shaped early seventeenth century Puritan and Baptist
communities and were reflected somewhat in other free
churches emerging in America later, particularly late
eighteenth century Methodists and early nineteenth century
Disciples of Christ.[1]

During the seventeenth and eighteenth centuries,
there were challenges and adjustments to this original
pattern; but it was only fully swept away in some churches
by the Second Awakening of the early nineteenth century
when "new means" were adopted to evangelize vast numbers
of unchurched persons. Adopted for revival circumstances,
the "new means" posited the preacher on a stage as the
central focus in a worship service devised to convert
the people in the congregation who were not yet eligible
to commune or give substantial shape to the preaching
and praying. (Lay exercise in prayer and exhortation
was encouraged by some nineteenth century revivalists
but usually for purposes that appear limited when compared
to such participation in the seventeenth and eighteenth
centuries.) The revivalists' major alterations in the
order and conduct of worship were made visible in the
internal architectural changes that gutted meeting houses
from the late 1820s until the Civil War. Removed were
the communion table and places for ministers and lay leaders to sit together near the people. And the eighteenth
century family box pews were replaced with slip pews so
that all the people faced forward to the newly erected
high platform where the preacher presided throughout the
worship. Often the choir and organ (if any) were moved
from the back balconies onto the same front platform with
the preacher to present a series of prayers, anthems, and
preaching to convert individuals. This study ends with
1835; for that year is seen as the watershed of revivalist
changes in worship as encouraged by the publication of
Charles Grandison Finney's Lectures on the Revivals of

Religion and numerous conversions in meeting house architecture.

The changes were even more profound than appear from
the alterations in order, conduct, and architecture of
worship. Clearly communion and substantive lay participation in prayer and preaching declined. But while a
sermon remained in the worship service, its scope narrowed. With the sermon focused on converting individuals,
a range of wider social and political concerns received
less attention from the pulpit and in the people's exhortations and prayers. Even those ministers who continued
preaching on wider issues were frustrated by the changes
in worship; for exercise of lay questioning and witnessing (and the reconciliation of frequent communion afterwards) had facilitated the opening of controversial matters in the sermon.

The importance of understanding changes in these
patterns is evident when we recognize that many twentieth
century free churches worship in the forms of nineteenth
century revivalists. In a chapter insightfully titled
"Behind the Current Stalemate," James F. White noted:

> The consequences for church architecture were much
> more far-reaching than are usually realized. Not
> only did revivalism lead to a new liturgical arrange-
> ment but eventually to a quite new concept of the
> basic purposes of a church building.[2]

Worship forms and architectural forms have their consequences for the shaping of church and society. As I have
detailed elsewhere, those who were trained to stand and
question their ministers in worship did not sit quietly
before Royal governors.[3] Reared so their presence made
a difference in worship where they could change what was
said and done, they changed the course of history as well.
Similar patterns of lay participation were supported for
different reasons in each denomination. Puritan theology
stressed the lay speaking as a check on ministers who
as all creatures would sin. Later, Methodists and Disciples of Christ stressed the lay practices to honor the
Spirit in all. Earlier, Separatists and Baptists had

stressed both reasons. The consequences of altering
worship forms invite further research; for instance when
I served as volume editor of Page Smith's Religious Origins of the American Revolution (Missoula, Scholar's
Press, 1976), he speculated that elimination of public
confession and other checks on authority in early nineteenth century American worship is a background for the
inability of many prominent twentieth century politicians
to confess their errors and crimes.

     While many intriguing questions lie beyond the scope
of this study, it aims to provide a sufficient understanding of sources and contours in early American free church
worship order and conduct so that others will see the
possibilities to do many dissertations needed on the
worship of specific denominations in each region and
period. For instance, we know that communion was very
frequent in seventeenth and eighteenth centuries and
infrequent as churches developed in the nineteenth century; but we do not know fully enough when and how such
changes occurred across the country. Extension of churches to minister to an expanding population occasioned the
change of practice in many instances. The majority of
churches thought ordained ministers must lead communion;
and in the expansion era of the early nineteenth century,
ministers with several charges could reach each church
only once a quarter or once a month at most. Laity served
the leadership needs of many churches who rarely saw an
ordained minister. Hence, weekly or even monthly communion became unknown or unfamiliar before thousands of
churches were sufficiently strong to have the services
of a full time minister. The alternative response to the
shortage of ordained clergy was to have weekly communion
celebrated by lay church leaders or by "irregularly"
ordained ministers. Such a response animated some Methodist and German Reformed communities in the late eighteenth century. In the nineteenth century, the Disciples
of Christ began with weekly communion led by laity not

because ministers were lacking but because of a strong
theological stress on the priesthood of all believers.[4]
As noted earlier, the revivalist emphasis of many churches
precluded frequent communion. And in some locations, a
minister's changing theological tastes altered the sacrament's frequency. Additional causes for the decline
of communion may emerge as needed dissertations on worship
are written.

Chapter One describes the morning order of worship
among Puritans in early seventeenth century America; and
Chapter Two describes their afternoon worship. Chapter
Three traces the distinguishing features of such worship
order back to their origins in the Separatist patterns
at Plymouth and forward to their continuation among the
Baptist churches and Quaker groups in seventeenth century
America. Chapter Four explores continuity and change
of worship order in seventeenth, eighteenth, and early
nineteenth centuries with some attention to the emergence
of worship among Methodists and Disciples of Christ.
Chapter Five describes developments in the imagery of
American worship from 1620 to 1835 not only in sermons
but also in the arts which are promising research subjects
that have only begun to inform ways we understand past and
present American worship. In that final chapter, we note
shifts in the conceptions of covenant that relate to
shifts in worship imagery and order. The conception of
God's covenant with the people became a covenant with
the remnant which gave way to a covenant with the individual.

Those familiar with ministers' liturgical duties
in the twentieth century will note the absence of chapters dealing with weddings and funerals (services that
preoccupy many contemporary clergy.) To distinguish
themselves from Catholics and Anglicans and primarily
to assert their belief that only baptism and communion
were sacraments, the earliest free church ministers in
America would rarely attend weddings or funerals much

less offer prayer or lead such services. The dead figured
in the Sunday sermons of the weeks after funerals; and
notices and confessions were given in Sunday worship weeks
before weddings.

As free churches developed into the eighteenth century, more ministers not only took an active role in weddings and funerals that competed for the attention they
had devoted more exclusively to Sunday worship but also
moved some features of worship (e.g. lay questioning of
ministers) out of the Sunday worship services and into
mid-week educational events in their homes as noted in
chapter four. Both developments not only weakened the
minister's and laity's focus on Sunday worship but also
lessened active lay leadership in Sunday worship. The
reintegration of church educational programs and Sunday
worship that has been occurring through 1970s and 1980s
witnesses to the way worth is given to those persons and
activities included in worship. Our contemporary clergy
and laity may profit from observing how early American
free church worship integrated many functions that are
scattered in the programs of many twentieth century
churches.

I

MORNING WORSHIP ORDER

IN JOHN COTTON'S PURITAN NEW ENGLAND

Boston's Puritan patriarch, John Cotton, provided
the most comprehensive description of seventeenth century
American free church worship with publication of The True
Constitution of a Particular Visible Church Proved By
Scripture (London, 1642) and The Way of the Churches of
Christ In New England (London, 1645). Other Puritan
leaders rightly acknowledged the Plymouth Separatists
as a source for the Bay Colony worship order, although
John Cotton minimized that connection when writing to the
English attempting to purify the Anglican church and not
separate from it. The Separatist order appealed to Puritans because John Robinson (the Plymouth community's
pastor in Leyden) had based each aspect of it on practices in the Old and New Testaments, the first century
synagogue and church, and the mid-week prophesying meetings so cental to the developing thought of many late
sixteenth and early seventeenth century Puritans and
Independents in England and on the continent. These same
sources informed emerging seventeenth century Baptist
and Quaker worship and would influence similar forms of
worship in Methodist societies a century later. After
detailing Cotton's worship order in these first two chapters, we will trace its seventeenth century origins and
offspring in the third chapter.

JOHN COTTON'S ORDERING OF WORSHIP

An extensive section from The True Constitution of
a Particular Visible Church Proved By Scripture conveys
Cotton's full order of worship. (In parentheses appear

19

the scriptural warrants Cotton cited in the margin of
the text.)[1]

> Quest. How is the public worship of God to be
> ordered, and administered in the Church?
> Answ. All the Members of the Church being met
> together as one man (Ezek. 46.10; I Cor. 11.33)
> in the sight of God (Act. 10.33) are to join togeth-
> er in holy duties with one accord (Deut. 4.24; I
> Cor. 14.16) the men with their heads uncovered and
> women covered (I Cor. 11.4-6).
> Quest. What part of public worship is first to be
> administered?
> Answ. The Apostle exhorteth that first of all:
> All manner of prayers be made for all men, for Kings,
> and all in authority, that we may lead a quiet and
> peaceable life, in all godliness and honesty (I Tim.
> 2.1-2; Ezra 6.10).
> Quest. Whither are set forms of public worship,
> devised and ordained by men an acceptable worship
> unto the Lord?
> Answ. If such set forms had been an ordinance of
> the Lord, and a worship acceptable to him, the Lord
> himself, or at least some of the Apostles, or Pro-
> phets, would not have held back that part of God's
> Counsel from the Church (Act. 20.26,27). Besides,
> public prayer is as well a part of public Ministry,
> as Prophesy is (Gen. 2.7; Neh. 8.6; I Cor. 14.16)
> and the forms of one might as justly be taught, by
> the precepts of men as the other (Isa. 29.13) and
> both of them are alike the gifts of the Holy Ghost,
> to whom it belongeth as well to teach us what to
> pray, as how to pray (Rom. 8.26) nor will it well
> stand with the holy gesture of Prayer, which is to
> lift up our eyes to Heaven (John 11.41 and 17.1)
> to cast down our eyes upon a Book (Ps. 121.1 and
> 123.1).
> Quest. What part of public worship is next to be
> administered?
> Answ. Before Prophesying it will be seasonable to
> sing a psalm (2 Kin. 3.15; Coll. 3.16) and by some
> of the Teachers of the Church to Read the Word,
> and therewith they Preach it, by giving the sense,
> and applying the use (Neh. 8.8; Act. 15.21; Luke
> 4.21, 23-28). In dispensing whereof the Minister
> was wont to stand above all the people in a Pulpit
> of wood and the elders on both sides (Neh. 8.4,5)
> while the people harkened unto them with Reverence
> and attention (Neh. 8.5; Luke 2.29) where there be
> more Prophets, as Pastors and Teachers, they may
> Prophesy two or three (Neh. 8.7; I Cor. 14.29) and
> if the time permit, the Elders may call any other
> of the Brethren, whither of the same Church or any,
> to speak a word of Exhortation to the people (Act.
> 13.15; I Cor. 14.31) and for the better edifying of

a manself or others, it may be lawful for any
(young or old) save only for women, to ask questions
at the mouth of the Prophets (Luke 2.46; I Cor.
14.35).

Quest. After the Ministry of the Word, what parts
of God's public worship is next to be administered?
Answ. After the Word (which is the Covenant of
God) the Seales of the Covenant are next to be administered; Baptism, and the Lord's Supper (Act.
16.14; 15.31,32,33) and as for Baptism, it is to
be dispensed by a Minister of the Word (Mat. 28.19)
unto a Believer professing his Repentance and his
Faith (Act. 8.36,37; Mat. 3.6) being a member of the
same Church Body (I Cor. 12.13) as also unto his
seed (Gen. 17.23; Act. 8.26,37; Act. 16.15,33; I
Cor. 7.14) presented by the Parent to the Lord and
his Church (Luke 2.12) at which time the Minister
in God's room calleth upon the parent to renew his
Covenant with God for himself and his seed (Gen.
17.1,2,3,7,8) and calleth upon God as the nature
of the Ordinance requireth for the pardon of original sin, and for the sin of the parents and for a
blessing upon the Sacrament and Infant (Mat. 3.11;
I Tim. 4.5) and then calling the child by the name
which the Parent hath given it for his own edification and the childs (Luke 1.59-63 and 2.21) he bap-
tiseth it either by dipping (Mat. 3.16; John 3.33;
Act. 8.38; Rom. 6.40) or sprinkling (I Cor. 10.2;
Heb. 20.22) into the name of the Father, the Son,
and the Holy Ghost.

Quest. How is the Lord's Supper to be administered?
Answ. The Supper of the Lord is to be dispensed by
the Minister of the Word (I Chr. 30.'17 and 25.5,6)
unto the faithful of the same body (I Cor. 10.17
and 12, 13, 14) or commenced to them by a like body
(Rom. 16.1,2) having examined and judged themselves
(I Cor. 11.28-31) and sitting down with him at the
Lord's Table (Mat. 26.20; Luke 22.27-30) before whom
the Minister taketh the bread and blesseth it, break-
eth it, and giveth it to the brethren with this commandment once for all, to take and eat it, as the
body of Christ broken for them, and this do in remembrance of him, in like manner also he taketh the cup,
and having given thanks, he poureth it forth, and
giveth it to them, with a commandment to them all,
to take and drink it as the blood of Christ shed for
them, and this also to do in Remembrance of him
(Mat. 26.26,27,28; Luke 22.19,20; I Cor. 11.23,24,
25) and after all thanksgiving is ended with singing
a Psalm (Mat. 27.30; Mark 14.26).

Quest. After the Ministry of the Word and the Seales
thereof, how is the Collection for the Saints to be
administered?
Answ. The Collection for the Saints was by the
Apostles Ordinance to be made: for the time every
Lord's day (I Cor. 16.1,2; Deut. 16.16) for the

measure as God had prospered every man (I Cor. 16.2; 2 Cor. 8.3) for the manner, not of constraint but freely (2 Cor. 9.5,7) brought by the givers as an offering to the Lord and laid down (Act. 4.34,35; Mark 12.42; I Chr. 19.17) as at first before the Apostles, so afterwards by their appointment, before the Deacons of the Church, as into a common Treasury (Act. 4.35; I Cor. 16.2) by them to be distributed to the supply of the Ministry and of the poor Saints according to their need and of all the outward Service of the Church (I Tim. 5.7,8; Gal. 6.6; Act. 5.35 and 6.1,2,3; Rom. 15.26).
Quest. What duty of God's worship is to be performed in dismissing the assembly?
Answ. After all parts of God's public worship have been performed by the Minister (Num. 6.23) or any of the Prophets is to dismiss the Assembly with a word of blessing: offering up blessings unto the Lord (I Kings 8.15) and putting a blessing upon the people (2 Sam. 6.18; I Kin. 8.55-56; Num. 6.23-27; 2 The. 3.17,18; 2 Cor. 13.14).
Quest. In what manner are all duties of God's worship to be administered?
Answ. In Spiritual simplicity without affectation of legal shadows (John 1.26) of worldly pomp or carnal excellence (2 Cor. 1.17 and 18.22; I Cor. 2.1, 2 and 6.13), decently (I Cor. 14.40) and in order (I Cor. 14.40) and to edification (I Cor. 4.26).[2]

In The Way of the Churches of Christ in New England, Singing of Psalms A Gospel Ordinance, and other writings, Cotton elaborated parts of the worship. He made clear that no particular order was necessary; but the pastor was under Apostolic injunction to maintain order in each of the parts of the worship service: I Corinthians 14.40 "provideth that all the ordinances of God, whether prayer, or prophecy, or singing of Psalms, or tongues, or interpretations, be all of them done decently, without uncomeliness, and orderly, without confusion..."[3] Order (to allow edification and correction of the congregation in all things) was repeatedly stressed by Cotton; for Puritan and Separatist practices were repeatedly criticized for cultivating disrupters of established English order in both church and state.

OPENING PRAYERS OF THANKSGIVING AND INTERCESSION

An early New England observer and critic, Thomas
Lechford, wrote, "The Pastor begins with solemn prayer
continuing about a quarter of an hour."[4] John Cotton
described the long period of opening prayers by the pastor:

> First then when we come together in the Church,
> according to the Apostle direction, I Tim. 2.1 we
> make prayers and intercessions and thanksgivings
> for ourselves and for all men, not in any pre-
> scribed form of prayer, or studied liturgy, but
> in such a manner as the Spirit of Grace and of
> prayer (who teacheth all the people of God, what
> and how to pray, Rom. 8.26,27) helpeth our infirmi-
> ties, we having respect therein to the necessities
> of the people; the estate of the times, and the work
> of Christ in our hands.[5]

All stood for prayer with hands lifted above their heads
in the Biblical manner enjoined in I Timothy 2.8; and the
prayers were all extemporaneously spoken whether by the
pastor, teacher, or others. It was not until the beginning of the eighteenth century and the establishment of
Brattle Street Church that even the Lord's Prayer was
used in Puritan related church worship; for "set forms
of prayer" were not considered true public prayer though
they might be used in private meditation and study.
Any of the worshippers (men or women) could "put up a
note" with the prayer concern. Such concerns were usually
written down on a piece of paper and posted on the church
door or given to the pastor or other church leader before
the service.[6]

SINGING OF PSALMS

All stood to sing a psalm before (and sometimes
after) the time devoted to opening of scripture, sermon,
exhortations, and questions.[7] As some of the psalms have
as many as 130 lines and would take 15 minutes to sing
(and twice that long if lined out),[8] there would be a
psalm both before and after the word only if they were
short psalms. The Psalms were sung in order throughout

the year and were not selected to fit with the preacher's
subject matter. While the Ainsworth Psalter was in con-
stant use at Plymouth throughout the century and for a
brief time at Puritan Salem, the Sternhold and Hopkins
Psalter (printed in the back of their bibles) was used
in Cotton's Boston church until 1640 when The Bay Psalm
Book translation became available.[9] With texts in hand,
the educated could sing the psalms to a limited reper-
toire of familiar tunes for which a deacon set the pitch.[10]
Lining out (a common later practice where the congregation echoed the deacon's reading or singing out of the
psalm line by line) was allowed by Cotton under certain
conditions:

> We for our parts easily grant that where all have
> books and can read, or else can say the Psalm by
> heart, it were needless there to read each line
> of the Psalm beforehand in order to singing. But
> if it be granted, which is already proved, that the
> Psalms to be ordinarily sung in Public are Scripture-
> Psalms, and those to be sung by the body of the
> Congregation, then to this end it will be a neces-
> sary help that the words of the Psalm be openly
> read before hand, line after line, or two lines
> together, that so they who want either books or
> skill to read may know what is to be sung and join
> with the rest in the duty of singing.[11]

There was neither unanimity about singing psalms
in worship nor was there what we would recognize as uni-
son singing. In 1650, John Cotton had strongly defended
the singing of psalms and some other Old Testament texts
by all in the congregation including women.[12] But a year
later John Spurre was excommunicated from Cotton's church
for, among other things, questioning "singing of psalms.[13]
And six years later Sister Hogg was excommunicated for,
among other things, "disturbing the Congregation by her
disorderly singing."[14] Other issues such as claims of
special revelation from God led to the excommunications;
but the citations indicate problems in psalm singing.
Cotton did not allow musical instruments or choirs in
public worship, two devices that would improve singing
in the eighteenth century.[15] While he allowed solo or

group singing of psalms to the playing of musical instruments as he allowed some dancing in the home, no organ
appeared in First Church of Boston until 1785.[16] And
seating together the most skillful singers was not explored until 1758 and not approved until 1761; and such
seating even then was not to allow a choir but rather
to rectify congregational singing.[17] Individuality of
expression within congregational singing had wide lati-
tude in the seventeenth century even if Thomas Walter
engages hyperbole in describing seventeenth century Psalm
singing that continued into the eighteenth century as
"like five hundred tunes roared out at the same time."[18]

READING AND EXPOUNDING AND PREACHING THE WORD

> After prayer, either the Pastor or Teacher, readeth
> a Chapter in the Bible, and expoundeth it, giving
> the sense, to cause the people to understand the
> reading, according to Neh. 8.8. And in sundry
> Churches the other (whether Pastor or Teacher) who
> expoundeth not, he preacheth the Word, and in the
> afternoon the other who preached in the morning doth
> usually (if there be time) read and preach and he
> that expounded in the morning preacheth after him.[19]

Cotton notes that there was no dumb reading of scripture;
for the reading of scripture included expounding. In
expounding to aid understanding, the reader of scripture
would make brief comments between the lines of scripture
and extended comments immediately before and immediately
after the scripture reading. There was no uncommented
upon reading of scripture in American free church worship
until Brattle Street Church began such practice in the
eighteenth century. The practice of simply reading the
scripture in worship without contiguous comment was considered dumb reading that would not speak; for either
the people would misunderstand important parts or cease
listening as an entire chapter was read. An alternative
of reading less than a chapter of scripture was similarly
rejected because it might lead to misuse of scriptures
out of context. When Cotton writes about "reading scripture" in the public worship of his church, he does not

always mention "expounding"; but in such instances, one
may be assured that such expounding was included in the
reading. Expounding could be broader than exegesis and
included exposition; for instance, John Winthrop records
the following example of Cotton expounding in a period
when fighting with Indians (as well as internal fighting
between Cotton and Pastor John Wilson) concerned Boston
and the wider Bay Colony churches and civil authorities
in August, 1637:

> Mr. Cotton, expounding that in 2 Chron. ... the
> defection of the ten tribes from Rehoboam, and his
> preparations to recover them by war, and the pro-
> phet's prohibition, etc., proved from that in
> Numbers 27.21, that the rulers of the people should
> consult with the ministers of the churches upon
> occasion of any war to be undertaken, and any other
> weighty business, though the case should seem never
> so clear, as David in the case of Ziglag, and the
> Israelites in the case of Gibeah, Judges, etc.[20]

Because exegesis of a sort was done during the reading of scripture in worship, one may find little exegesis
in some printed sermons of seventeenth and eighteenth
century preachers in the new world, although many published sermons combine what was said in reading and expounding with what was said in preaching. John Cotton's
sermons were not written until after they had been
preached. Cotton and most of his colleagues dispensed
even with notes in the pulpit. Cotton Mather names John
Warham (minister at Dorchester and later at Windsor) as
the first to read sermons in New England; for Warham could
not summon his powers. But Warham's way was disdained.[21]
And Cotton argued, "All the work that reading could reach
unto, could not reach to beget and work saving faith,
which is the principal scope of preaching."[22] And to
Mr. Balls, he noted, "I have known a Minister to edify
the people more by silence in the pulpit through strength
of temptation, than ever I knew any to do by Reading a
Homily upon the Book."[23]

During the sermon, members of the congregation took
notes. From these, parents would later question their

children on the matter of the sermon. From such notes,
small study groups later in the week would discuss the
sermons with both those who had been present and others
who had been unable to be present. And such notes were
the basis for later published volumes of the ministers'
sermons. The living ministers usually were allowed to
correct the transcript of the sermon before it was published; but sometimes such courtesy was not shown the
clergy. For instance, in 1642, Winthrop notes:

> Now came over a book of Mr. Cotton's sermons
> upon the seven vials. Mr. Humfrey had gotten
> the notes from some who had took them by
> characters [i.e. a shorthand], and printed
> them in London, he had 300 copies for it, which
> was a great wrong to Mr. Cotton, and he was
> much grieved at it, for it had been fit he
> should have perused and corrected the copy
> before it had been printed.[24]

Although the extensive preaching was usually delivered by ordained ministers, laity did the preaching in
churches that had no ordained clergy. For instance,
deacon William Brewster preached regularly at Plymouth
church; and in Boston's first church, lay leaders were
designated by the pastor John Wilson to do preaching
when he was sailing back to England for a time in 1631:

> Mr. Wilson, praying and exhorting the congrega-
> tion to love, etc., commended to them the exer-
> cise of prophecy in his absence, and designed
> those whom he thought most fit for it, viz.,
> the governor, Mr. Dudley, and Mr. Nowell, the
> elder.[25]

And with Wilson in England in 1635, the lay activity in
preaching was evident even though John Cotton was preaching also: "Mr. Cotton preached out of Numbers xxxv.13,
and one of the members taught out of that in Lamentations
iii.39; Wherefore doth a living man complain?"[26] And
Winthrop had preached even outside his own congregation.
On April 3, 1634, "the governor went on foot to Agawam
[Ipswich] and because the people there wanted a minister,
spent the Sabbath with them, and exercised by way of
prophecy, and returned home the 10th."[27]

EXHORTING AND QUESTIONING BY LAITY

After preaching and returning to his seat, the ordained or lay leader of worship called upon "any other
of the Brethren whither of the same Church or any, to
speak a word of Exhortation to the people."[28] It was
not necessary that the person exhorting be a member in
good standing; for instance, in 1643 Samuel Gorton, im-
prisoned for writing letters condemning church ordinances
and other church practices, was given time to exhort
after one of John Cotton's sermons even though it was
clear that Gorton deviated greatly in viewpoint:

> The next Lord's day in the forenoon, the prisoners
> would not come to the meeting, so as the magistrates
> determined they should be compelled. They agreed
> to come, so as they might have liberty after sermon
> to speak, if they had occasion. The magistrates'
> answer was, that they did leave the ordering of
> things in the church to the elders, but there was
> no doubt but they might have leave to speak, so as
> they spake the words of truth and sobriety. So in
> the afternoon they came, and were placed in the fourth
> seat right before the elders. Mr. Cotton (in his
> ordinary text) taught then out of Acts 19. of Deme-
> trius pleading for Diana's silver shrines or temples,
> etc. After sermon Gorton desired leave to speak,
> which being granted, he repeated the points of Mr.
> Cotton's sermon, and coming to that of the silver
> shrines, he said that in the church there was nothing
> now but Christ, so that all our ordinances, minis-
> ters, sacraments, etc., were but men's inventions
> for show and pomp, and no other than those silver
> shrines of Diana. He said also that if Christ
> lived eternally, then he died eternally...[29]

His words do not appear to have affected his later con-
viction in court which was based on his statements in
letters and under examination; but as we will note later,
some Quakers who used the exhortation time without permission to express their views were convicted for disturbing worship. That some Puritan churches continued
the exhortation time, in spite of what they saw as abuses
of it, shows the importance with which it was viewed.
And it usually allowed strong disagreements to be aired
in worship in an orderly way, although the conflict with

Pastor John Wilson led some laity to interrupt and challenge the pastor in the middle of his sermon.[30]

The time of exhorting was accompanied by questioning
of the minister on the matter of the sermon. Before coming to the new world, English Puritans and Continental
Independents had regularly engaged in such exercises as
part of the weekday Bible study sessions called prophesying. Away from Anglican liturgical services, some Independents on the continent included the exercise of the
prophesyings in Sunday worship services. The Separatists
at Plymouth were such a group; and the Bay Colony Puritans had followed them in such a practice for worship.
Such times in worship were aimed to learn the truth that
may or may not have been adequately expressed by the
preachers and exhorters:

> Neither are they that speak in the exercise of
> prophecy to make a sermon by the hour glass...;
> that, were to abuse the time and wrong the gifts
> of others; but briefly speak a word of exhorta-
> tion as God enableth, and that, after the minis-
> terial teaching be ended, as Acts xii, questions
> also about things delivered, and with them, even
> disputations, as there is occasion, being part,
> or appurtenances of that exercise. I Cor. xiv.35,
> Acts xvii.2, Acts xviii.4.[31]

While the Separatists in Leyden and Plymouth allowed even
women to speak out in worship to exhort when extraordin-
arily moved to do so, they did not allow women to ask
questions in worship. But the Puritans of Boston allowed
only males to exhort and ask questions; although women
were free (within limits established in the Anne Hutchinson case) to join in prophesyings, exhortations and
questions in study meetings at private homes during the
week.

The widespread practice of exhortations and questions
in worship of the Bay Colony is witnessed by assembly
resolutions and sermons aimed to regulate such practice.
With "all teaching elders through the country"[32] present
at a synod called at Newton in 1643, the following re-
solves were debated and passed:

>   1.   That though women might meet (some few to-
>   gether) to pray and edify one another; yet such
>   a set assembly (as was then in practice at Boston)
>   where sixty or more did meet every week, and one
>   woman (in prophetical way, by resolving questions
>   of doctrine, and expounding scripture) took upon
>   her the whole exercise, was agreed to be disorderly,
>   and without rule.
>
>   2.   Though a private member might ask a question
>   publicly, after sermon, for information; yet this
>   ought to be very wisely and sparingly done, and
>   that with leave of the elders: but questions of
>   reference (then in use,) whereby the doctrines were
>   reproved, and the elders reproached, and that with
>   bitterness, etc. was utterly condemned.[33]

The resolutions were occasioned by controversies around
Anne Hutchinson (controversies that some of her Boston
followers carried into neighboring meeting houses) as
Winthrop notes in the February prior to the September
synod called to deal with disturbances: "the members
of Boston (frequenting the lectures of other ministers)
did make much disturbance by public questions, and ob-
jections to their doctrines, which did in any way disagree from their opinions...."[34] Thomas Weld used more
graphic language:

>   Now after our Sermons ..., you might have seen
>   half a dozen Pistols discharged at the face of
>   the preacher ... so many objections made by the
>   opinionists in the open assembly against the
>   doctrine delivered.[35]

That the prophesying exercise in public worship survived
the controversies around Anne Hutchinson is further witnessed by the synod sermon delivered by Ezekiel Rogers
of Rowley at Cambridge, June 8, 1647: "He reproved also
the practice of private members making speeches in the
church assemblies to the disturbance and hindrance of the
ordinances...."[36] But Rogers' attack on such lay speaking in worship was not well received; and no synod action
was taken to discourage such prophesying.[37] General
Court legislation passed in 1653 to restrain lay preaching was quickly repealed after protests by clergy with
petitions from several towns. Major concern expressed
in such protests was opposition to civil government

interfering with church affairs.[38]

CELEBRATING THE LORD'S SUPPER

Cotton wrote of "celebrating" the Lord's Supper and noted they administered it "once a month at least" in the Sunday morning worship.[39] "After the celebration of the Supper, a Psalm of thanksgiving is sung, (according to Mat. 36.30) and the church is dismissed with a blessing."[40] (In the afternoon service, there were baptisms and admission of new members along with offerings, confessions, and censures concluded by singing of a psalm and a benediction.)[41] With interpolations against practices of kneeling or love feasts (which he saw as unwarranted by scripture), Cotton gave his most extensive description of Lord's Supper in The Way of the Churches of Christ in New-england:

> Both the Sacraments we dispense, according to the first institution, Baptism to Disciples, and (who are included in them) their seed. The Lord's Supper to such as neither want knowledge nor grace to examine and judge themselves before the Lord Such as lie under any offence publicly known, do first remove the offence, before they present themselves to the Lord's Table; according to Mat. 5.23, 24. The members of any Church, if any be present, who bring Letters testimonial with them to our Churches, we admit them to the Lord's Table with us; and their children also (if occasionally in their travel they be borne with us) upon like recommendation we admit to Baptism. The prayers we use at the administration of the seales, and not any set forms prescribed to us, but conceived by the Minister, according to the present occasion, and the nature of the duty in hand. Ceremonies we use none, but are careful to administer all things according to the primitive institutions....

> In time of solemnization of the Supper, the Minister having taken, blessed, and broken the bread, and commanded all the people to take and eat it, as the body of Christ broken for them, he taketh it himself, and giveth it to all that sit at Table with him, and from the Table it is reached by the Deacons to the people sitting in the next seats about them, the Minister sitting in his place at the Table.

> After they have all partaken in the bread, he
> taketh the cup in like manner, and giveth thanks
> a new (blesseth it), according to the example of
> Christ in the Evangelist, who describes the insti-
> tution Mat. 26.27, Mark 14.23, Luke 22.17. All
> of them in such a way as setteth forth the Elements
> not blessed together, but either of them apart;
> the bread first by itself, and afterwards the wine
> by itself; for what reason the Lord himself best
> knoweth, and we cannot be ignorant, that a received
> solemn blessing expressly performed by himself, does
> apparently call upon the whole assembly to look a-
> gain for a supernatural and special blessing in
> the same Element also as well as in the former;
> for which the Lord will be again sought to do it
> for us.[42]

John Cotton denied Lechford's charge that most Bay
Colony churches dismissed non-members before communion,
although Lechford had taken care to note that "Anyone,
though not of the Church, may, in Boston, come in, and
see the Sacrament administered, if he will."[43] Cotton
wrote:

> It is not true that we hold out any at all, English
> or Indian, out of our Christian Congregations. All
> without exception are allowed to be present, at our
> public Prayers and Psalms, at our reading of Scrip-
> tures, and the preaching and expounding of the same,
> and also at the admitting of Members and dispensing
> of seales and censures.[44]

It is difficult to judge which account is more accurate;
for while Lechford tried to maximize offensive practices
of a New England he wished to discredit by association
with the most extreme Separatist ways, Cotton tried in
The Way of Congregational Churches Cleared and The Keyes
of The Kingdom of Heaven to minimize especially such
practices that would be unpalatable to English Puritans
who remained within the Anglican church. There is no
doubt that all new arrivals from England had to be admitted to a New England church membership before qualifying for the Lord's Supper, no matter what their standing
with any church in England. But qualifications such as
regeneracy were muted in Cotton's apologetic accounts
as in similarly motivated accounts by John Davenport and
Richard Mather.[45] "The Church" referred to members, those

qualified to eat the Lord's Supper; and "the congregation" referred to all others in the worship service.
Uncontroversial matters in Lechford's description of
a Lord's Supper may add to our accurate information on
some Bay Colony church worship, if not the Boston church:

> Once a month is a Sacrament of the Lord's Supper,
> whereof notice is given usually a fortnight before,
> and then all others departing save the Church, which
> is a great deal less in number than those that go
> away, they receive the Sacrament, the Ministers and
> ruling Elders sitting at the Table, the rest in
> their seats, or upon forms: All cannot see the
> Minister consecrating, unless they stand up, and
> make a narrow shift. The one of the teaching Elders
> prays before, and blesseth, and consecrated the
> Bread and Wine, according to the words of Institu-
> tion; the other prays after the receiving of all
> the members: and next Communion, they change turns;
> he that began at that, ends at this: and the Min-
> isters deliver the Bread in a Charger to some of
> the chief, and peradventure gives to a few the Bread
> into their hands and they deliver the Charger from
> one to another, till all have eaten; in like manner
> the cup, till all have drunk goes from one to an-
> other. Then a Psalm is sung, and with a short bless-
> ing the congregation is dismissed.[46]

TIMING OF THE WORSHIP SERVICE

According to Lechford, the morning worship began
at around nine o'clock.[47] And although the length of
the morning worship would depend on the number of concerns
raised for prayer at the beginning and for discussion
after the sermon as well as the length of the sermon,
two or three hours would be likely for the order outlined.
(One could have done the order in half that time if prayers, psalms, exposition, sermon, exhortations and questions, and Lord's Supper were succinct. But there was
no idolatry of an hour as the length for worship in the
seventeenth century.) From materials already cited, the
opening prayer was fifteen minutes by Lechford's observation; and the singing of two or three psalms (one or two
around the opening of the word and another at the end of
the worship) would take twenty minutes to a half hour by

Curwen's calculations or twice that long if lined out. Reading a chapter of scripture with expounding could easily take fifteen minutes. The preaching, exhorting, and questioning probably took between one and two hours. Celebrated monthly at least, the Lord's Supper could add a half hour to the service. So, worshipping three hours in the morning would not be unusual.[48]

II

AFTERNOON WORSHIP ORDER

IN JOHN COTTON'S PURITAN NEW ENGLAND

The main difference between morning and afternoon
worship was that lay questioning and witnessing that
followed the morning sermon was replaced by lay speaking
that informed examinations of those presented for baptism,
church membership, confession, admonition, or excommunication. Such lay speaking was curtailed in later years
as some ministers absorbed such examinations into the
preliminary hearings held at other public and private
forums noted in chapter four. As with morning lay witnessing, women were allowed to speak out for examinations
in Separatist afternoon worship; but they were not allowed
to speak out in most Puritan afternoon worship. Puritan
women could present their written confessions or testi-
monies and have ministers or other men read them aloud
in afternoon worship.

SETTING AND ORDERING OF AFTERNOON WORSHIP

After two in the afternoon, they repair to the
meeting-house again; and then the Pastor begins,
as before noon, and a Psalm being sung, the Teacher
makes a Sermon. He was wont, when I came first, to
read and expound a Chapter also before his Sermon
in the afternoon. After and before his Sermon,
he prayeth.

After that ensues Baptism, if there by any, which
is done, by either Pastor or Teacher, in the Deacon's seat, the most eminent place in the Church,
next under the Elder's seat. The Pastor most commonly makes a speech or exhortation to the Church,
and parents concerning Baptism, and then prayeth
before and after. It is done by washing or sprinkling. One of the parents being of the Church, the
child may be baptized, and the Baptism is into the
name of the <u>Father</u>, and of the <u>Son</u>, and of the <u>holy
Ghost</u>. No sureties are required.

Which ended, follows the contribution, one of the
Deacons saying, Brethren of the congregation, now
there is time left for contribution, wherefore as
God hath prospered you, so freely offer. Upon some
extraordinary occasions, as building and repairing
of Churches or meeting houses, or other necessities,
the Ministers press a liberal contribution, with
effectual exhortations out of Scripture. The Magistrates and chief Gentlemen first, and then the Elders,
and all the congregation of men and most of them
that are not of the Church, all single persons,
widows, and women in absence of their husbands,
come up one after another one way, and bring their
offerings to the Deacon at his seat, and put it
into a box of wood for the purpose, if it be money
or papers; if it be any other chattle, they set
it or lay it down before the Deacons, and so pass
another way to their seats again. This contribution is of money, or papers, promising so much money:
I have seen a fair gilt cup with a cover, offered
there by one, which is still used at the Communion.
Which monies, and goods the Deacons dispose towards
the maintenance of the Ministers, and the poor of
the Church, and the Church's occasions, without
making account ordinarily.

But in Salem Church, those only that are of the
Church, offer in public; the rest are required to
give to the Ministry, by collection, at their houses.
At some other places they make a rate upon every
man, as well within, as not of the Church, resid-
ing with them, towards the Church's occasions; and
others are beholding, now and then, to the general
Court, to study ways to enforce the maintenance
of the Ministry.

This done, then follows admission of members, or
hearing of offense, or other things, sometimes till
it be very late. If they have time, after this is
sung a Psalm, and then the Pastor concludeth with
a Prayer and a blessing.[1]

Lechford's foregoing description of afternoon worship
order corresponds to the brief information Cotton sup-
plies; but there was some variation between the manner
of worship in Boston and some other towns.

Marian Card Donnelly's definitive study, The New
England Meeting House of the Seventeenth Century, notes
that interior arrangements are not known for meeting
houses of 1630 through 1642; and little is known from
seventeenth century records about the interior arrangements from 1642 to 1700. Statements about seventeenth

century internal worship settings in America are largely
conjecture inferred from arrangements in seventeenth
century English churches or eighteenth century American
meeting houses.[3] When Lechford noted that the deacons'
seat was the most eminent place "next under the Elder's
seat" we do not know whether "under" refers to height
architecturally or stature ecclesiologically. In Cotton's
Boston, the deacons' seat was no higher than all the
other pews on the floor; although Cotton noted that in
some other meeting houses the deacons' seat was lifted
up higher than the others. Cotton mentions no separate
pew for elders or pastor. He wrote that the deacons
"sit in a seat under the Elders"; but the expression
comes in a sentence where the preaching is discussed;
so, the phrase may mean nothing more than that the deacon's seat was placed in front and below the pulpit.[4]
From the celebration of the Lord's Supper, we know there
was a table at the deacons' seat and that there was room
for the pastor and teaching elder and ruling elders to
sit at that table with the deacons. There is no evidence
whether the table was free standing or attached to the
deacons' seat.[5] During Cotton's days, there were usually
two deacons of the Boston church; and in addition to the
pastor and teacher (often referred to as elders), there
was at least one lay ruling elder.[6] Because "elder"
referred to ordained ministers as well as to an elected
lay person in some churches, references to the seating
of the meeting are further obscured. But if one must
give some conjectures about internal arrangements, then
the most likely seventeenth century pattern would be one
akin to their contemporary English Puritan places of
worship described by Horton Davies:

> They emphasized the co-ordinate importance of Word
> and Spirit, so that the preaching of the Word and
> the celebration of the "Gospel Sacraments" (Baptism
> and Lord's Supper) required in Puritan assemblies
> for worship a centrally placed pulpit, usually on
> the long wall of a rectangular-shaped church, and
> beneath it a Communion table centrally placed sur-
> rounded by a pew in which the elders or deacons

sat, and a font (usually rather inconspicuous).[7]
Introduction of ministerial pews behind the pulpit came
in the eighteenth century when the meeting houses were
expanded to accommodate many more people.[8]

BAPTIZING THE CHILDREN

Lechford's foregoing order of the afternoon worship
describes the baptism practice more fully than Cotton's.
But Cotton notes in addition that the Father presented
the child if he was a member; and there were to be no
God parents. He explained that the child was baptized
by right of the parent's Covenant;[9] and at one baptism,
he noted that the father's presenting of the child was
"the father's incentive for the help of his faith...."[10]
During his ministry at Boston from October 10, 1633 to
his death on December 23, 1652, 1034 children were baptized in the Sunday afternoon worship services.[11] And
church records further show that there were baptisms in
about half of the Sunday afternoon worship services during Cotton's tenure as teacher of the Boston church.
Most children born to members were presented for baptism
at the first Sunday service after their birth; although
a good number were presented at the second Sunday after
their birth. One finds a few older children baptized;
but usually their parents had not been church members
at these children's births. In one instance, we have a
glimpse from church records of two parents' promises:
"John Stockbridge and Anne his wife promising in the face
of the Church, to bring up their said Child under the
Ordinances of Christ, in some Church gathered and Ordered
according to Christ."[12]

OFFERING AT THE DEACON'S SEAT

To the deacons' seat at the Lord's Table, members
brought their children for baptism; and to same place,

one person from each worshipping household brought forward offerings during each Sunday afternoon worship.
Cotton gave this description of the offering that followed
the preaching and baptism (if any):

> the Deacons ... do call upon the people, that as
> God hath prospered them, and hath made their hearts
> willing, there is now time left for contribution:
> presently the people from the highest to the lowest
> in sundry Churches do arise, the first pew first,
> the next next, and so the rest in order, and pre-
> sent before the Lord their holy offerings. For
> in the old Testament at their solemn feasts none
> was to appear before the Lord empty. Deut. 16.16.
> And the Lord's day is only unto the Christians the
> ordinary solemn feast of the Lord: in the new
> Testament the Christians laid down their oblations
> at the Apostles' feet (Acts 4.35) into whose place,
> for that service, Deacons were substituted, Acts
> 6.3.[13]

As already noted in Lechford, all men came forward as
did women who were single, widowed, or married to men
not present. They placed money, papers promising money,
or other gifts in the deacons' wooden box. While churches
in New Haven and elsewhere may have received some unsigned
papers, libelous verses, gloomy Quaker messages, and bad
money in the box in the seventeenth century, Boston
church records reveal no such problems until 1752 when
the church began requiring all persons to sign even the
money they placed in the box.[14]

Deacons were elected by the church members and ordained by the laying on of hands. According to the 1648
Cambridge Platform of which John Cotton was a chief ad-
viser, the office was "limited unto the care of the tem-
poral good things of the church, it extends not to the
attendance upon, and administration of the spiritual
things thereof, as the word and sacraments, or the like."
And the deacons were to spend the monies to supply "the
Lord's Table, the table of the ministers, and of such
as are in necessity to whom they are to distribute in
simplicity."[15] Contrary to Lechford's assertion, the
deacons were required at times to render account of their
administration; and dismissal from office for malfeasance

was not unknown among seventeenth century New England
Puritans.[16]

ADMITTING, ADMONISHING, AND CASTING OUT MEMBERS

A major portion of the afternoon worship was devoted
to hearing confessions of faith and sin from those who
wished to join the church or to retain their membership
that was in jeopardy. Such proceedings occurred in from
one-third to a half of the Sunday afternoon worship services each year of Cotton's ministry to First Church
Boston. During those nineteen years, 652 individuals
were admitted to the church membership; and twenty-nine
individuals were excommunicated. Of the twenty-nine,
fifteen were never restored to membership; but eight
made acceptable confession, regained their membership,
and retained it without further incident. Of the remaining six, each was excommunicated two or three times; so,
the total number of admissions and excommunications is
slightly larger than the number of individuals involved.
In addition, five persons were admonished but repented
before the more severe step of excommunication was taken.[17]
While the extensive lay participation in morning worship
was expressed distinctively through the opening prayers
and the later exhortations and questions following sermons, the lay participation in afternoon worship was
evidenced in the often extensive rehearsals of their
spiritual life histories followed by the questions and
comments from other laity.

Thorough examination of a prospective member was
usually conducted by the ministers and the lay ruling
elders days or even weeks before he or she was presented
for admission in public worship; and they publicly announced the candidate's name before such examination so
that anyone with a reservation could tell the elders.
The Cambridge Platform detailed the minimal norms to

become a member:

> The things which are requisite to be found in all
> church members are <u>repentance</u> from sin and <u>faith</u>
> in Jesus Christ; and therefore these are the things
> whereof men are to be examined at their admission
> into the church, and which then they must profess
> and hold forth in such sort, as may satisfy rational
> charity that the things are there indeed.

> ...The weakest measure of faith is to be accepted
> in those that desire to be admitted into the church,
> because weak christians, if sincere, have the sub-
> stance of that faith, repentance and holiness, which
> is required in church members; and such have most
> need of the ordinances, for their confirmation and
> growth in grace. The Lord Jesus would not quench
> the smoking flax, nor break the bruised reed, but
> gather the tender lambs in his arms and carry them
> gently in his bosom. Such charity and tenderness
> is to be used, as the weakest christian, if sincere,
> may not be excluded nor discouraged. Severity of
> examination is to be avoided.

> ...In case any through excessive fear, or other
> infirmity, be unable to make their personal rela-
> tion of their spiritual estate in public, it is
> sufficient that the elders having received private
> satisfaction, make relation thereof in public be-
> fore the church, they testifying their assents there-
> unto: this being the way that tendeth most to edi-
> fication. But where persons are of greater abili-
> ties, there it is most expedient that they make
> their relations and confessions personally with
> their own mouth, as David professeth of himself.

> ...A personal and public confession, and declaring
> of God's manner of working on the soul, is both
> lawful, expedient and useful, in sundry respects,
> and upon sundry grounds.[18]

The same requirements are detailed for members from other
churches and those baptized children who had grown up in
the church.

When Cotton was admitted to the Boston Church membership in afternoon worship September 8, 1633, "he signified his desire and readiness to make his confession
according to order, which he said might be sufficient
in declaring his faith about baptism" about which he
elaborated with reference to his own son Seaborn. "He
desired his wife might also be admitted a member, and
gave a modest testimony of her, but withal requested,

that she might not be put to make open confession, etc.,
which he said was against the apostle's rule, and not
fit for women's modesty." He allowed the elders might
examine her in private; but they simply asked her if
she consented to the confession of faith he had made and
desired admission. After her affirmation, they were
both admitted by the vote of the church.[19]

While Cotton encouraged a woman to write out her
profession of faith to be read aloud by the elders in
worship with her assent, other churches encouraged women
to speak out their account. For instance, John Fiske
reported in 1644 how the Wenham church allowed such
speaking out as submission and not an exercise of power:

> Some agitation was about women making their rela-
> tions in public, occasioned from the practice of
> some churches to the contrary where the officers
> (as was said) and four or five of the members
> appointed to the purpose were to hear the same and
> testify thereof to the church, the same being taken
> down in writing by the officers from her mouth and
> related to the church. As for the considering that
> place in I Cor. 14, women not to speak &c., to
> the scripture it was resolved to speak by way of
> teaching a prophecy, as it seems the scope of this
> place, and such a speaking argues power. And so
> the parallel place seems to expound it in I Tim. 3.
> Whereas it was objected, but to ask a question in
> public they may not so much as do that, as expressed
> by the text ask your husband at home. Answered,
> asking of questions (imparts power also) in the
> church, but this kind of speaking is by submission
> where others are to judge &c. and to the glory of
> God, as Deborah, Mary, Elizabeth, Anne &c. And
> resolved that they should make their relations per-
> sonally in public; grounds, because the whole church
> is to judge of their meetness which cannot so well
> be if she speak not herself.[20]

Fiske made detailed entries on some of the public
"relations" (the person's own accounts of his or her
regenerating experience). George Norton's "relations"
was a tour through the minds of mid-seventeenth century
New England theologians:

> This day being the Lord's day the letters from the
> church at Gloucester were read concerning George
> Norton's dismission and his relations required.
> He accordingly does. He was convinced on the very

acting of some evil and of the guilt in that regard and brought to some reformation and to some
civility. He set upon reading and to some profit
and to some desire of good. For which he chose the
way to this country and after that come hither feeling with the best....explanations and joined with
the church at Salem, though there he made not his
rest. After going to Plymouth he fell into Armin-
ianism and held from free will. But he set upon
it to read Dr. Preston's "God's All Sufficiency"
which again settled &c. After coming to Salem again
he read ... and then convinced of an evil, but shame
confessed so as could not discover. Afterward he
fell to some loathing of it yet often fell into the
sin again. Then Jer. 2:22, could not look for mercy,
and the place seconded by that scripture, the dog
returned to his vomit &c. He could not see which
was God could show one mercy. Reading of Byfield
tended more to his misery than his comfort; he could
not see that God could be just and he receive mercy.
Yet considered who the author of mercy &c. and came
to consider maybe God might show mercy. Upon which
the... ...taken off when he cast himself upon God,
though he could not see how.

Next that he reads was Mr. Williams, things very
pleasing but not reaching his condition. After
occasionally to baptism and with Mr. Cotton. What
way to use to get from under the spirit of bondage?
Asked, as God said, by casting self upon Him. Then
He replied with many promises and that in Mat. 11:28,
which I could not fend off. Coming to Salem, then
some deadness. Afterward in the spring going to
Mr. ... to work he went to hear Mr. Hooker in Can-
bridge whose way was to answer a question in all
the particulars if knew it. Touching the guilt
of ... salvation. And troubled in the night he was
minded to look at Psalms 124:7; rose to look at
it and found it to suit him. Upon this concluded
that he was in a good estate and grew serene. This
before he heard Mr. Hooker preach something from
Jer. 31, I'll forgive iniquity. After, this query,
how do I know that I profess in Christ? Answer,
that in John 1:1, Christ is the word so as cannot
receive the word kindly. Yet stick at that. Best
promise from Mat. 11:28; the rest settled from
Psalm 77, that stick ye yet not a purpose. This
one sealed up at the Supper from these words, those
that come to me I'll in no wise cast off. This
his state, that setting so to speak of that which
rest from God's glory some revolt &c. as in the case
of some vow that was made to God which a just pro-
vocation of God whereupon there kindness ye met,
better not to vow than not to perform. Thereupon
then ... the performing &c. and this God answered.

> Upon questioning he testified his judgment in church
> government in baptism of infants &c. and his assents
> to confession of faith, that touching deacons ex-
> cepted as ourselves. The covenant then administered
> to him.[21]

On an earlier occasion in the same church, Anne Fiske,

the wife of James Fiske, spoke out her relations which

reveal a well educated mind. After a person's relations,

there were usually questions from church members; but

after her speaking, there were no questions:

> Anne Fiske was called forth to declare what God had
> done for her salvation in bringing her to Christ &c.
> She delivered first her grounds of a second relation
> and that she could do it in faith from divers pas-
> sages in Psalms 71. She was first convinced (at
> 12 years of age) by a sermon on Psalms 32:1 discov-
> ering to her by misery while she was still unpar-
> doned. Her particular sins were foolishness, vanity,
> and pride. This continued for divers years and was
> further followed, however, some seven or eight years
> after by divers sermons of Mr. Rogers of Dedham on
> Romans 3:13-14. So went on till Mr. Rogers came
> in his course of preaching to preach of that in
> Romans 3:24. Whereupon he, pressing the necessity
> of believing in the Lord, opened her heart to choose
> by faith in Christ (whereas before she rested on
> performances). Now her heart set to seek some faith
> &c. That scripture much help secured, Isa. 43:24,
> they bought me no sweet cane &c., so that decision
> [?] partly from necessity of believing from God's
> command to believe, partly that He pardons for His
> own name's sake.
>
> Temptations. First about the truth of humiliation
> taken off of Mr. Roger's handling on a sermon from
> Romans 4. touching Abraham protesting that he had
> nothing to glory of, ye wouldest something to glory
> of in the flesh then wouldest bring your humiliation
> &c. And so of a passage of Mr. Hopkins, not of any
> works lest any boast. And reading Mr. Colver's
> view of faith and in respect of church covenant
> that passage, look not from qualifications or such
> a measure of humiliation &c. the Lord offers Christ
> freely.
>
> Second that she should not persevere, to that Mr.
> Rogers in Romans 5:2, by whom also we have access
> by faith into this grace wherein we stand, whereupon
> declaring how only such in Christ stands and of the
> probability [?] of faith. His reasons: kept by
> the power of God it duly with Christ should be kept;
> that tis the will of God that all the further have
> given Christ (but her stick being whether God were

willing); he that hath begun will persist.

Third that she was a hypocrite because greatly af-
flicted: to that the consideration of what David
held forth of himself in Psalms 73 whereby it appeared affliction was not that ground or note of
hypocrisy.

In coming to New England the hearing of opinions
in New England (when in ship) some discouraged and
meeting with them at Boston and in some meetings
there finding they did only envy us the godly ministers here this made her the more willing to come
to Salem, which was a place more free. And when
at Watertown she heard oft that the church was more
strict about receiving members. Yet she was willing to come thither but whereas in public their
small trials and only about circumstances it was
such a trouble as if had been against her. Join
she would not for the present.

After joined immediately with smallpox. Then concerned if the Lord would try though his sister did
not. So he did and did also help and to that end
brought that place in Deut. 30:5. This Mr. Peters
preaching urging then their want of growth touched
her... ...since upon ... there were to be ... and
... ... her ... [five words illegible] would ...
...that were about the same time given notice of.
Seeking God was answered from that scripture, Christ
comes to take away sin and to dissolve the work of
the devil. Which these answered and also about
subscription to that in Isa. 1:19. Other trials
to that in Isa. 1:27. And two things especially
when she was near death: what would become of her
children if she died and to that, this consideration
she may live and be no help to them; and, the fruits
of God's mercy how to endure it and be fit for it.
To that II Cor. 5:1.[22]

While these Puritan churches had statements of faith
or covenants, to own the covenant on admission to membership was not synonymous with subscribing to such written
documents. With reference to the Salem church, Nathaniel
Morton noted in 1669:

The Confession of Faith and Covenant forementioned,
was acknowledged only as a Direction pointing unto
that Faith and Covenant contained in the holy Scripture, and therefore no man was confined unto that
form of words, but only to the Substance, End and
Scope of the matter contained therein: And for the
Circumstantial manner of joining to the Church, it
was ordered according to the wisdom and faithfulness

> of the Elders, together with the liberty and abil-
> ity of any person. Hence it was, that some were
> admitted by expressing their Consent to that writ-
> ten Confession of Faith and Covenant; others did
> answer to questions about the Principles of Religion
> that were publicly propounded to them; some did
> present their Confessions in writing, which was
> read for them, and some that were able and willing
> did make their Confession in their own words and
> way.23

In the 1630s, all such procedures were conducted in the
Salem Sunday afternoon worship; but in the 1640s, the
speaking out by women was shifted to a weekday followed
by their assenting to the covenant in Sunday worship.24
Salem's pastor John Higginson affirmed in 1665 that a
confession of faith "is to be looked upon as a fit means
whereby to express ... their Common Faith and Salvation,
and not to be made use of as an imposition upon any."25
And John Cotton gave a theological understanding to
"covenant of grace" that shows why it could not be synonymous with even the whole of scripture much less any
written church covenant:

> Let not men be afraid, and say, That we have no
> revelation but the word: for I do believe, and
> dare confidently affirm, that if there were no
> revelation but the word, there would be no spiri-
> tual grace revealed to the soul; for it is more
> than the Letter of the Word that is required to
> it: not that I look for any other matter besides
> the word.   But there is need of greater light,
> then the word of itself is able to give; for it
> is not all promises in Scripture, that have at
> any time wrought any gracious changes in any soul,
> or are able to beget the faith of God's Elect:
> true it is indeed, whether the Father, Son, or
> Spirit reveal any thing, it is in and according
> to the word; but without the work of the Spirit,
> there is no faith begotten by any promise.26

Although First Church of Boston would develop more
elaborate covenants at the end of the seventeenth century, its first covenant of August 27, 1630 was drafted
in simple form as the church met at Charlestown:

> In the Name of our Lord Jesus Christ, and in
> Obedience to His holy will, and Divine Ordin-
> ance:

We whose names are hereunder written, being by

His most wise, and good Providence brought together
into this part of America in the Bay of Massachusetts, and desirous to unite ourselves into one
Congregation, or Church, under the Lord Jesus
Christ our Head, in such sort as becometh all those
whom He hath Redeemed, and Sanctified to Himself,
do hereby solemnly, and religiously (as in His
most holy Presence) Promise, and bind ourselves,
to walk in all our ways according to the Rule of
the Gospel, and in all sincere Conformity to His
Holy Ordinances, and in mutual love, and respect
each to other, so near as God shall give us grace.[27]

A more detailed covenant was adopted by the Salem Church
in 1636. The numbered statements date back in substance
to the August 6, 1629 covenant; but the first part of
the preamble was an addition:

Gather my Saints together unto me that have made
a Covenant with me by sacrifyce. Psa: 50:5

We whose names are here under written, members of
the present Church of Christ in Salem, having found
by sad experience how dangerous it is to sit loose
to the Covenant we make with our God: and how apt
we are to wander into by paths even to the losing
of our first aims in entering into Church fellowship: Do therefore, solemnly in the presence of
the Eternal God both for our own comforts and those
which shall or may be joined unto us renew that
Church covenant we find this Church bound unto at
their first beginning. vitz: That we Covenant with
the Lord and one with another, and do bind our selves
in the presence of God, to walk together in all his
ways according as he is pleased to reveal him self
unto us in his Blessed word of truth. And do more
explicitly in the name and fear of God, profess
and protest to walk as followeth through the power
and grace of our Lord Jesus.

1. first we avow the Lord to be our God, and our
selves his people in the truth and simplicity of
our Spirits

2. We give our selves to the Lord Jesus Christ,
and the word of his grace, for the teaching, ruling
and sanctifying of us in matters of worship, and
conversation resolving to cleave to him alone for
life and glory; and oppose all contrary ways, can-
nons and constitutions of men in his worship.

3. We promise to walk with our brethren and sisters
in the Congregation with all watchfullness, and
tenderness avoiding all jelousies, suspicions, back
bitings, conjurings, provokings, secret risings of
spirit against them, but in all offences to follow

the rule of the Lord Jesus, and to bear and forbear give and forgive as he hath taught us.

4. In public or private, we will willingly do nothing to the offence of the Church but will be willing to take advice for ourselves and ours as occasion shall be presented.

5. We will not in the Congregation be forward either to show our own gifts or parts in speaking or scrupuling or there discover the failing of our brethren or sisters but attend an orderly call there unto; knowing how much the Lord may be dishonoured, and his Gospel in the profession of it, slighted by our distempers, and weaknesses in public.

6. We bind ourselves to study the advancement of the Gospel in all truth and peace, both in regard of those that are within, or without, no way slighting our sister Churches, but using their Counsell as need shall be; not laying a stumbling block, before any, no not the Indians, whose good we desire to promote, and so to converse, as we may avoid the very appearance of evil.

7. We hearby promise to carry ourselves in all lawful obedience, to those that are over us in Church or Common weale, knowing how well pleasing it will be to the Lord, that they should have encouragement in their places, by our not grieving their spirits through our irregularities.

8. We resolve to prove our selves to the Lord in our particular callings, shunning idleness as the bane of any state, nor will we deal hardly, or oppressingly with any, wherein we are the Lord's stewards also.

9. promising to our best ability to teach our children and servants, the knowledge of God and his will, that they may serve him also and all this, not by any strength of our own, but by the Lord Christ, whose blood we desire may sprinkle this our Covenant made in his name.[28]

And the Westminster Confession of Faith was in large part commended to the churches by the 1648 Cambridge Synod representing twenty-eight of the twenty-nine churches.[29]

Although covenants or statements of faith often would be included in Sunday afternoon worship services when new members were admitted, their use in worship was not limited to those occasions: for instance, John Fiske read the Wenham church statements of faith in the Sunday

service when he announced there would be administration
of the Lord's Supper on the following Sunday.[30] And
church wide renewal of the covenant occurred in some
churches: Salem church experienced the 1636 renewal
already cited and 1662 and 1680 renewals inspired by
Pastor Higginson's perceptions of the 1662 and 1679 New
England Synods.[31]

Cotton no doubt practiced gentleness in the "trial"
of those seeking admission. "In this trial we do not
exact eminent measure, either of knowledge or holiness,
... for we had rather ninety-nine hypocrites should per-
ish through presumption, than one humble soul belonging
to Christ should sink under discouragement or despair."[32]
But Increase Mather and others found an "unjustifiable
severity" in requirements for oral declaration of faith
and repentance before the whole congregation.[33] Even
the prospect of private examination procedures before
the most eminent leaders of the community could understandably discourage some persons, especially young men
and women who were eligible to apply at age fourteen or
fifteen.[34]

While most churches applied the same procedures
to members transferring from other New England churches
as they did to those newly arrived from England or those
joining a church for the first time, First Church of
Boston often accepted members from other New England
churches without public inquiry and required relations
in private only so long as they brought proper letters
of dismissal from their former church.[35] What made a
proper letter of dismissal was debated in Rev. John
Fiske's church; and it was decided to refuse letters
signed only by the elder of the church from where the
person came. The letter needed to reflect a dismissal
action by the whole church; for "some are under offence
and the offence is known only to some but not wise from
elders; some are of corrupt judgment; maybe the elders
are corrupt too."[36] Similarly, while the Boston church

allowed visiting persons to eat the Lord's Supper if they
presented letters indicating membership in another New
England Puritan church, Rev. Fiske's church thought such
letters neither "safe nor sufficient seeing such letters
may be counterfeited...."[37] At that Wenham (Clemsford)
church, the verbal testimony of one or more local church
members sufficed to allow the seale of the Supper to a
visiting church member. The need for proper letters of
dismissal in order to join another church gave churches
influence over the moving of their members as the Cambridge Platform made clear: "It is therefore the duty
of church members ... to consult with the church whereof
they are members about their removal, that accordingly
they having their approbation, may be encouraged, or
otherwise desist."[38] If there were charges of sinfulness, the letters would be refused until the person was
cleared or confessed and forgiven so as to be a member
in good standing. Just reasons for moving away included
persecution, probable future sinfulness, or lack of ade-
quate subsistence in the person's hometown. The person
was to receive the benefit of the doubt when asking to
move with the letter of dismissal and was not to be forci-
bly detained.[39]

CASTING OUT AND ITS CAUSES

The procedures for casting out members (sometimes
called excommunication) were similar to those for admitting members. In a private hearing, elders and a few
others would be involved as witnesses if the persons
offending and offended could not resolve their differences. If no resolution were possible in private, the
lay ruling elder usually propounded the matter to the
whole church; and following statements and questions,
the church would vote for the lay ruling elder or pastor
to clear, admonish, or cast out the person. Part of the
proceedings could occur at mid-week meetings and part

in Sunday afternoon worship. To admonish a person was
a half way step that suspended the person from the Lord's
Supper; but if the person repented and made acceptable
confession, then he or she was restored to the Lord's
Supper. Those who remained obstinate were excommunicated;
and if they later repented, they needed to go through
all the steps of examination required of new members.
"But if the offense be more public at first, and of a
more heinous and criminal nature ... then the church,
without such gradual proceeding, is to cast out the of-
fender from their holy communion...."[40] We will examine
in detail which causes were seen as heinous as well as
which causes were most frequently the subject of discussion in First Church Boston worship. Whatever the sin,
the excommunicated could continue to worship in the congregation but without benefit of the sacraments. And
although excommunication was explicitly not to deprive
the person of any civil rights, church members were to
refrain from all possible contact (including eating and
drinking) with the excommunicated except for necessities
of domestic and civil relations: e.g. a child or wife
could eat with an excommunicated man of the house.[41]

Excommunication usually resulted from the offending
party refusing to come before the church trial or failing to make a full confession. Hence, a charge of lying
or withdrawing from fellowship was often added to the
original charge. Of the fifteen persons excommunicated
once and never readmitted at First Church Boston during
John Cotton's ministry, nine were charged with persisting in what we would call theological or ecclesiological
attitudes which led several of them to speak evil of
church authorities. Anne Hutchinson and some of her
followers were examples of this category. She was cast
out in 1638 as was Judith Stone three weeks later and
Philip Harding a year later. (Mrs. Harding had persisted
in asserting Anne Hutchinson's innocence.) Anne's
own son, Francis,was cast out in 1641 for calling the

church a whore among other things. In 1646, Sarah Keaynes
was cast out for irregular prophesying and refusing to
come to regular worship; and then in 1651, John Spurre,
Richard Lippincott, Ann Burden, and Nichlis Upsall were
cast out for withdrawing communion and attacks on church
authority.[42] The six others permanently excommunicated
were Anne Walker (1638 excessive drinking, beating her
children, and lying), Richard Turner (1638 excessive
drinking), Anne Hibbon (1640 persisting in false charges
that another person's rates were too high), Nathaniel
Partridge (1644 committing perjury), Nicholis Charlett
(1646 stealing), and James Smith (1647 committing adultery and lying).[43]

Eight other excommunicated persons were readmitted
to membership from five to twenty-one months after being
cast out. All but one of these cases occurred between
1640 and 1646. The exception was the first person excommunicated from First Church: Robert Parker was cast out
in 1635 for the economic sin of oppressing his wife's
children by selling away their inheritance; but he was
readmitted after five months. The long periods between
excommunication and readmission were experienced by Thomas
Marshall (twenty-one months after a 1644 excommunication
for bad dealing and lying in business), Simon Bird
(twenty-one months after a 1646 excommunication for dallying with his maid servant), Edward Bates (eighteen months
after a 1643 excommunication for dallying with another's
wife, stealing, and lying), Henry Dawson (fourteen months
after a 1645 excommunication for committing of adultery),
and Anne Hett (eleven months after a 1642 excommunication
for blaspheming and drowning attempt on her child).
Shorter periods were experienced by Zacheus Bosworth
(five months after a 1643 excommunication for excessive
drinking) and John Underhill (six months after a 1640
excommunication for committing of adultery, self justifying, and reviling the governor and magistrates).[44]

Six additional excommunicated members were readmitted

only to be excommunicated again. Two of these were admitted a third time and continued in the church without
further incident: and one was not readmitted. Two others
of the six were admitted a third time and later excommunicated a third time. And the last of the six was excommunicated three times but admitted four times so as to
end his life with church membership. The latter, Richard
Wayte, was excommunicated in 1638 for purloining material
sufficient for three men's gloves from material entrusted
to him, readmitted in 1640, excommunicated two months
later for dissembling at his readmission by not confess-
ing his sinful practices with Lester Gunton, readmitted
in 1641, excommunicated in 1670 for repeatedly drinking
to excess, and readmitted six months later.[45] Some of
the others evidenced long periods of being excommunicate.
John Hurd was cast out for repeated drunkenness in 1649,
readmitted in 1652, cast out for the same offense in
1653, readmitted in 1664, and cast out for the same sin
a final time in 1666.[46] William Lytherland was excommunicated for drunkenness in 1670, readmitted in 1674, and
cast out a final time for drunkenness in 1680.[47] William
Francklyn was excommunicated for cruel correction of his
servants in 1645, readmitted in 1646, excommunicated two
months later for deception and extortion in his iron work,
readmitted in 1652.[48] Arthur Clark was one of the more
inventive persons to be excommunicated. In 1644, lay
ruling elder Thomas Oliver made the following entry of
an October 27 church action:

> One brother Arthur Clark was in open Assembly by
> our Elder Mr. Oliver with Consent of the Church
> by their silence Cast out of it for scandalously
> stealing many gallons of wine out of a pipe of
> wine, and corrupting the rest by filling it up
> with beer and also stealing wine out of other
> vessels partly selling of it and with part thereof
> distempering himself unto drunkenness and like-
> wise for extenuating his falsehood therein with
> some lying.[49]

He was readmitted a year later and excommunicated for
drunkenness in 1656.[50] The last of the six occasioned

on February 23, 1639/1640 the longest excommunication
entry in the records of First Church:

> James Mattock, cooper, by our pastor (in the Name
> of the Lord and with the Consent of the Church,
> taken by their silence) Cast out of the Church for
> these Scandals Committed by him, partly in Old
> England and partly in New England.
>
> In old England, 1. For that he denied Conjugal
> fellowship unto his wife for the space of two
> years together upon pretense of taking Revenge
> upon himself for his abusing of her before marri-
> age, and also for the avoiding of Charge by Child-
> ren of her, when as yet he very suspiciously and
> offensively frequented the Company of one Whit-
> taker's wife all that time, and gave her 2s a week
> towards her maintenance, yea so obstinately Continu-
> ing therein as that the Magistrate of Bristow Im-
> prisoned him in Newgate prison there for ten days
> and her the said Whittaker's wife in Bridwell there.
>
> 2. For that in Old England after his profession
> of Religion he was known to be sundry times drunken,
> and so ragingly overtaken therewith at one time,
> as that he offered unclean dalliance and filthy
> Carriage to a Certain maid in a victualing house
> openly.
>
> 3. In New England for that he was openly drunk 2
> times.
>
> Also for that from hence he hath sundry times writ-
> ten to the said Whittaker's wife for her Coming
> hither, and that having received 4 letters from
> her, and pretending to show her letters to the
> Elders, he brought them but 2 of the said 4 letters,
> and (as he said) burned the other wherein the [51]
> greatest evils betwixt them was suspected to be.

Readmitted in 1641 and then excommunicated for drunkenness and unnamed outrage on the Sabbath in 1649, he was
admitted for the third time in 1653 and thereafter remained a member in good standing.[52]

Five additional persons were admonished in worship
but were later reconciled by their confession and church
vote. As with excommunication, either the pastor (John
Wilson) or a lay ruling elder propounded the case and
pronounced the vote of the church to admonish or recon-
cile. Voting was either by silent consent to the pastor's
or ruling elder's suggestion (if there was no dispute of

the charges) or by show of hands where there was a division of opinion as rarely noted.[53] Only male church members voted. While Salem church voted by show of hands and abided by majority decision, First Church Boston attempted to decide all cases by unanimous consent. The latter procedure would prolong discussion or in a rare case lead to the admonishing of those who would not join the consensus. Winthrop noted that Anne Hutchinson's sons were admonished for obstructing the consensus in their mother's case.[54] First Church Boston records show no such admonishing; so, one may conclude there was more admonishing than church records indicate.

Admonition suspended the member's vote and participation in the Lord's Supper for from one month to eight months during the time John Cotton served the Boston church. Temperance Sweete was restored four weeks after contributing to the disorderly conduct of others by selling them too much to drink in 1640. John Webb was restored five weeks after feasting and sporting and absenting himself from the church fellowship during a day called for humiliation and prayer in 1639. Such reconciliations required the admonished to make open acknowledgment of their sinfulness. Longer periods of living under admonishment correlate to having committed sins against other persons: six months in the case of Robert Keayne (who sold wares at excessive rates in 1639), seven months in the case of George Clifford (who committed false dealing in promising more than he could deliver in 1645), and eight months in the case of John Pemberton (for unbrotherly contention and reviling speeches toward a John Baker).[55] In such cases, there were not only full confessions but also some restitution; for instance, the reconciliation of Robert Keayne noted "his penitential acknowledgment thereof this day and promise of further satisfaction to any that have just offense against him."[56]

PRAISING, THANKSGIVING, AND BLESSING

Although a closing psalm would be omitted if the hour was late as Lechford noted, John Cotton wrote that "after a Psalm of praise to God, with thanksgiving, and prayer to God for a blessing upon all the ordinances administered that day, and a blessing pronounced upon the people, the Assembly is dismissed."[57]

III

ORIGINS AND OFFSPRING

OF PLYMOUTH'S SEPARATIST WORSHIP ORDER

Governor John Winthrop described a Lord's Day with Separatist Plymouth Church which he and Boston's pastor John Wilson visited in October 1632:

> On the Lord's Day there was a sacrament, which they did partake in; and in the afternoon, Mr. Roger Williams (according to their custom) propounded a question, to which the pastor, Mr. Smith, spake briefly; then Mr. Williams prophesied; and after the governor of Plymouth spake to the question; after him the elder; then some two or three more of the congregation. Then the elder desired the governor of Massachusetts and Mr. Wilson to speak to it, which they did. When this was ended, the deacon, Mr. Fuller, put the congregation in mind of their duty of contributing; whereupon the governor and all the rest went down to the deacon's seat, and put into the box, and then returned.[1]

In the worship of Plymouth Church, we see not only practices but also persons who informed the worship of both the early American Puritans and Baptists. Plymouth's deacon Samuel Fuller practiced medicine and shared the worship forms with the arriving Puritans in 1629; and Plymouth's teaching elder Roger Williams carried some of these worship practices into the shaping of Baptist church worship in Rhode Island where he went in 1636 after two years at Plymouth and a time in Salem. That Puritans and Baptists followed Separatist worship practices is more understandable when we note that the practices synthesized by the Separatist's Leyden pastor John Robinson were largely drawn from the same sources that inspired all three groups: the New Testament and the mid-week prophesying meetings held in England and on the continent. After tracing Robinson's sources for worship, we note how such worship was related to practices

by other American free churches in the seventeenth century.

JOHN ROBINSON'S SHAPING OF PLYMOUTH'S WORSHIP

John Robinson shaped the practices of the Plymouth
Separatists not only as their pastor for ten years in
Leyden before they sailed for the new world but also by
pastoral letters from Leyden until his death in March
1625. Leyden church was derived from the Separatist
church founded in 1602 by John Smythe and Richard Clyfton
in William Brewster's home at Scrooby, England. Educated
at Cambridge with many other Puritans, Robinson joined
the Separatist Scrooby church in 1604; and after Clyfton
followed Smythe to Amsterdam, Robinson ministered to the
remaining church. In 1608, Robinson led the Scrooby
congregation to Francis Johnson's Amsterdam church that
Smythe and Clyfton had joined. But within a year, Robinson led a group to Leyden probably to avoid the controversies among Smythe, Clyfton, Johnson, and others in the
Amsterdam church split by Smythe's insistence on adult
believer's baptism and rejection of psalm singing. In
Amsterdam, Robinson met Henry Ainsworth who had ministered to the church with Johnson until Johnson's marri-
age. And Robinson agreed with Ainsworth's affirmation
of singing psalms in worship that appeared in print a
year later as a continuing argument with John Smythe:
"[we] do content ourselves with joint harmonious singing of the Psalms of Holy Scripture, to the instruction
and comforts of our hearts, and praise of our God."[2]
From Amsterdam, Robinson's Leyden congregation received in 1612 Ainsworth's The Book of Psalmes: Englished
both in Prose and Metre which was carried to Plymouth
seven years later and used in worship until the end of
the century. But music was not all that Robinson's church
received from Amsterdam to shape worship. The year Robinson and his congregation were in Amsterdam, the church of

John Smythe was worshipping in the following way:

> The order and government of our church is 1. we
> begin with a prayer, after read some one or two
> chapters of the bible, give the sense thereof, and
> confer upon the same, that done we lay aside our
> books, and after a solemn prayer made by the 1.
> speaker, he propoundeth some text out of the
> Scripture, and prophecieth out of the same, by
> the space of one hour, or three quarters of an
> hour. After him standeth up a 2. speaker and
> prophecieth out of the said text the like time
> and space, some time more and some time less.
> After him the 3. the 4. the 5. & as the time will
> give leave, Then the 1. speaker concludeth with
> prayer as he began with prayer, with an exhorta-
> tion to contribute to the poor, which collection
> being made is also concludeth with prayer. This
> morning exercise begins at eight of the clock and
> continueth unto twelve of the clock the like unto
> 5. or 6. of the Clock. Last of all the execution
> of the government of the church is handled.[3]

It is not certain that Smythe's 1608 pattern of worship
in Amsterdam reflected the pattern of worship at Scrooby;
for his Scrooby colleague Clyfton gave the following
description of worship at his Amsterdam church in 1612:

> 1. Prayer and giving of thanks by the pastor or
> teacher.
> 2. The Scriptures are read, two or three chapters,
> as time serves, with a brief explanation of their
> meaning.
> 3. The pastor or teacher then takes some passage
> of Scripture, and expounds and enforces it.
> 4. The sacraments are administered.
> 5. Some of the Psalms of David are sung by the
> whole congregation, both before and after the exer-
> cise of the Word.
> 6. Collection is then made, as each one is able,
> for the support of the officers and the poor.[4]

Robinson's worship pattern (later reflected in Plymouth
church worship and then Boston church worship) was a
synthesis of the Amsterdam worship patterns practiced
by the two original founders of the Scrooby church.
In 1610, John Robinson articulated an approach to worship that would include major lay participation whatever
the order:

> The officers of the church are to govern every
> action of the church, and exercise of the com-
> munion; are they therefore alone to do all things?
> They, if there be any of them in the church, are

> to govern in every election and choice of ensuing
> officers: are they therefore alone to choose, ex-
> cluding the church? They are to govern in preach-
> ing, prophesying, and hearing the word, and receiv-
> ing the sacraments, singing of psalms, distributing
> unto the necessity of the saints: are they there-
> fore alone to prophesy, to sing psalms, to contri-
> bute to the poor, and the rest? With as little
> reason can it be affirmed, that they alone are to
> have communion, in the censures to admonish, and
> judge, because they are to govern in the carrying
> and administering of those matters.[5]

Extensive sections of Robinson's writings argued
for the right of laity to join in the prophesying of
public worship. He filled pages with examples of such
lay exercise evidenced from Old and New Testament records of Jewish synagogue and early church worship.[6]
Such passages we have seen cited ten to twenty years
later by John Cotton's work justifying the New England
ways of worship. Citing the 1571 Embden synod action
urging churches to follow Paul's injunction of I Corinthians 14 so that all prophesy, Robinson noted, "we believe with the Belgic churches, that this exercise is
to be observed in all congregations, therefore we also
observe it in ours."[7] In arguing why the exercise was
needed in churches, Robinson gave added insight into how
the exercise was conducted to include disputations and
questions as well as added exhortation:

> The third foundation of this exercise is laid in
> the manifold, and the same most excellent ends
> attainable only by this means. 1. That "God may
> be glorified, whilest every one doth administer
> to another this gift which he hath received, as
> good dispensers of the manifold grace of God,"
> 1 Pet. iv. 10, 11. 2. That "the Spirit be not
> extinguished," 1 Thess. v. 19, 10, that is, the
> gift of prophecy, or teaching; in which it may so
> come to pass, that some in the church, though no
> ministers, may excel the very pastors themselves.
> 3. That such as are to be taken into the ministry
> of the church, may both become and appear "apt to
> teach." 1 Tim. i. 3. This seeing, the apostle
> would have done, he would questionless have some
> order for the doing of it; which, excepting this
> of prophecy, we have none of apostolical institu-
> tion. 4. That the doctrine of the church may be
> preserved pure, from the infection of error: which

is far more easily corrupted, when some one or two
alone in the church speak all, and all the rest have
deep and perpetual silence enjoined them. 1 John
iv. 1; Rev. ii. 2, 7, with i. 11. 5. That things
doubtful arising in teaching may be cleared, things
obscure opened, things erroneous convinced; and
lastly that as by the beating together of two stones
fire appeareth, so may the light of the truth more
clearly shine by disputations, questions, and an-
swers modestly had and made, and as becomes the
church of saints, and work of God. Luke ii. 40;
iv. 21, 22; Acts xvii. 2; xviii. 24, 26, 28. 6.
For the edification of the church, and conversion
of them that believe not: and this the rather because it appertaineth not properly to the pastors,
as pastors, to turn goats or wolves into sheep, but
rather to feed the flock and sheep of Christ, in
which the Holy Ghost hath made them overseers.
1 Cor. xiv. 4, 24, 25; Acts xx. 28. 7. And lastly,
Lest by excluding the commonalty and multitude from
church affairs, the people of God be divided, and
charity lessened, and familiarity and good-will be
extinguished between the order of ministers and
people.[8]

Robinson cited both positive and negative reasons for the
exercise: i.e. to allow everyone's insight to be shared
and to root out corruptions. Depending on their theology,
later groups would stress one or the other of those reasons for allowing laity to prophesy. Prophesying con-
sisted of both exhorting and questioning; while the former allowed each person to make their positive contribution to edify others, the latter provided the opportunity
to check against error. "[M]en though not in office,
have liberty to move, and propound their questions, and
doubts for satisfaction, as also having received a gift,
to administer the same, unto edification, exhortation,
and comfort."[9] Quakers in America appropriated only the
positive use of prophecy; but Roger Williams insisted on
both uses as noted at the end of this chapter.

Robinson also followed Smythe and others in the
emerging Baptist churches to urge the right of women
to prophesy in public worship.[10] He argued that Paul's
prohibition was against ordinary speaking but not against
extraordinary prophesying inspired by the Spirit. And
his argument noted that such extraordinary prophesying

by women was occurring in seventeenth century congregations:

> It is therefore most clear that the apostle aims
> not at all at any ceasing of the gift of extra-
> ordinary prophecy now going on, but at the uni-
> versal and absolute restraint and prohibition of
> women's prophesying, not extraordinary but ordin-
> ary.[11]

Hence, in Leyden and Plymouth church worship, women were
barred from asking questions (which was seen as ordinary
prophesying) but were free for exhorting (which was seen
as potentially extraordinary prophesying).

On administration of the sacraments, Robinson and
Smythe disagreed sharply and prefigured later crises in
American free church worship. While Robinson believed
that the covenant constituted the church, Smythe held
that baptism constituted the church. The implications
for worship were profound. Smythe came to believe that
until persons were properly baptized they could not pray
nor could the faithful pray with them; for to do so was
sin. For him, adult baptism became the proper mode; and
previous infant baptisms were invalid; and so, persons
joining his church were baptized even if they had already
experienced baptism in other churches.[12] Because Robinson believed that God's gift of the covenant constituted
the church and made the sacrament valid whatever the age
of the baptized, he recognized as sufficient the baptisms
in the Roman Catholic church as well as in the Church of
England.[13] Similarly, Robinson saw no sin in praying and
communing with those in the Church of England; and so,
some of his followers at the New England Plymouth church
worshipped in the Anglican church on occasional trips to
England. Such practices were among those prompting Roger
Williams to leave the Plymouth church in 1633; for his
views developed along the lines Smythe had earlier es-
poused.

While Smythe allowed laity to administer the sacraments in the absence of ordained ministers,[14] Robinson
did not. The Lord's Supper was a part of every Sunday

morning worship of Robinson's Leyden church; but the Plymouth church bemoaned their lack of sacraments before they ordained Ralph Smith pastor in 1629. In 1623, they noted with reference to sacraments:

> The more is our grief, that our pastor is kept from us, by whom we might enjoy them; for we used to have the Lord's Supper every Sabbath, and baptism as often as there was occasion of children to baptise.[15]

And in the same year, Robinson responded negatively to William Brewster's request to administer the sacraments in Plymouth in the absence of an ordained minister.[16]

As lay ruling elder at Plymouth, Brewster led worship and followed Robinson's rejection of set prayer forms (including the Lord's prayer).[17] But instead of leading a long prayer at the opening of the worship, Brewster gave short prayers throughout the worship service for reasons William Bradford recounted:

> He always thought it were better for ministers to pray oftener, and divide their prayers, than be long and tedious in the same (except upon solemn and special occasions, as in days of humiliation and the like). His reason was, that the heart and spirits of all, especially the weak, could hardly continue and stand bent (as it were) so long towards God, as they ought to do in the duty, without flagging and falling off.[18]

Differing from the French Reform practice, Robinson and Brewster led prayer with their heads uncovered.[19] The lay shaping of the prayers by passing notes to the worship leader probably derived from the Dutch practice common at the beginning of the seventeenth century. Such practice was also common among Scotch Presbyterians; but Horton Davies does not note the practice by any English churches until dissenter Richard Baxter used it near the end of the seventeenth century.[20] At the close of the leader's prayer in Robinson's churches, the people said "Amen" aloud as they could during scripture readings and sermons when strongly agreeing with what was said.[21]

Robinson urged that admonitions and excommunications be conducted as a part of public worship on the sabbath with all church members party to the proceedings:

> The administration ... being a part of the commun-
> ion of saints, and public worship, is to be per-
> formed on the Lord's day, as well as other parts
> are; and to be joined with the administration of
> the word, sacraments, alms, and the rest, as mak-
> ing all one entire body of communion....22

Robinson suggested that in some instances excommunication
would wisely be administered early in the worship so that
no notorious offenders would take communion. Laymen as
well as ministers could speak out during the admonishing
and excommunicating; and women joined in the voting by
silent consent.[23] Similar lay participation was allowed
when persons joined the church during worship.[24]

THE SEPARATIST SHAPING OF PURITAN WORSHIP

On May 11, 1629, Puritan leader John Endecott wrote
Plymouth's Governor Bradford:

> I acknowledge myself much bound to you for your
> kind love and care in sending Mr. Fuller among us,
> and rejoice much that I am by him satisfied touch-
> ing your judgements of the outward form of God's
> worship. It is as far as I can yet gather, no
> other than is warranted by the evidence of truth,
> and the same which I have professed and maintained
> ever since the Lord in mercy revealed himself unto
> me; being far from the common report that hath been
> spread of you touching that particular.25

A number of scholars have debated the extent to which Bay
Colony Puritans adopted Plymouth Separatist patterns of
church life and thought.[26] Some arguments are akin to
those used publicly by early Puritan leaders. In trying
to assure English backers of the New England enterprise
that Puritans were not following Separatist ways, John
Cotton stressed that any similarity of practices was
nearly coincidental:

> Neither did the church of Plymouth incontinently
> leaven all the vacinity...
> I do not know, that they agreed upon it by any
> common consultation: but it is true, they did as
> if they had agreed (by the same spirit of truth
> and unity) set up (by the help of Christ) the
> same model of churches, one like to another. But

whether it was after Mr. Robinson's pattern, is
spoken gratis; for I believe most of them knew not
what it was, if any at all. And if any did know
it, the men were such as were not wont to attend
to the patterns of men in matters of religion (for
against that many of them had suffered in our na-
tive country) but to the pattern of the Scriptures.[27]

But more privately, Cotton had counselled the Puritans
to learn from the Plymouth Colony; and Robinson had urged
the Plymouth church to cooperate fully with the Puritans.[28] The process by which Plymouth Separatists informed Bay Colony Puritan worship was best described by
Plymouth's Edward Winslow in 1646:

[S]ome of the chiefs of them advised with us (coming over to be freed from the burdensome ceremonies
they imposed in England) how they should do to fall
upon a right platform of worship, and desired to
that end since God had honored us to lay the foundation of a Commonweale, and to settle a Church
in it, to show them whereupon our practice was
grounded.

We accordingly showed them the primitive practice
for our warrant, taken out of the Acts of the
Apostles and the Epistles ... together with the
commandments of Christ, and for every particular
we did from the book of God. They set not the
Church at Plymouth before them for example, but
the Primitive Churches were and are their and our
mutual patterns and examples, which are only worthy
to be followed.[29]

When one examines worship practices and their justifications, one sees that the Bay Colony reliance on Robinson's Leyden and Plymouth church models was substantial.
In a Separatist Leyden church and not in Puritan English
churches were the roots of the distinctive elements in
early American worship (strong lay participation in shaping prayer, prophesying through exhortation and question,
and admitting and casting out members during the worship).
In the area of worship at least, William Rathband's seventeenth century observation is truer than most seventeenth century Puritans and twentieth century scholars
were willing to admit:

Master Robinson did derive his way to his separate
congregation at Leyden; a part of them did carry it

> over to Plymouth in New England where Master Cotton
> did take it up. ... [T]he most who settled their
> habitations in that Land did agree to model them-
> selves in Churches after Robinson's pattern.[30]

BEGINNING BAPTIST WORSHIP ORDER IN AMERICA

The earliest Baptist churches in America were founded
in Rhode Island by those who had been worshipping in the
Plymouth Separatist church and the Boston Puritan church.
Early Baptist worship orders were probably similar to
those observed in Plymouth and Boston with a few amend-
ments by deletion. Definitive determination of these
orders is made difficult by the absence of reliable
church records for the early years at the first Baptist
churches both at Providence and Newport. But internal
church disputes and later recorded changes of worship
add to our understandings from the founders' writings.
And the prosecution of Puritans who formed Baptist churches later in Boston and Kittery produced added evidence
of worship practices. Early American Baptists broke
from the Separatists and Puritans to assert a different
understanding of who were eligible to worship rather than
how they were to worship.

Edmund Morgan aptly styled Roger Williams' approach
to worship "The Equality of Worship."[31] For Williams,
every part of the worship service was an equally important ordinance of God; and so, one needed to meet the
qualifications for baptism and the Lord's Supper in order
to be present for prayers or preaching. In the 1644
Queries of Highest Consideration (identified by John
Cotton as Williams' work), Williams' position was dis-
tinguished from both the Church of England and the French,
Scotch, and Dutch Reform Churches:

> Since you both seem to magnify the Scales of Bap-
> tism and the Lord's Supper with a difference and
> excellency above other Ordinances, We Query where
> the Lord Jesus appoint such a difference and dis-
> tinction? And whether there was not as full Com-
> munion practiced by the first Christians in the

Word, Prayer, and Community, as in the breaking
of Bread? Acts 2.42[32]

During the same year in The Bloody Tenent of Persecution,
Williams attacked some of the New England ways of John
Cotton:

> whatever such an unbelieving and unregenerate per-
> son acts in Worship or Religion, it is but sin,
> Rom. 14. Preaching sin, praying (though without
> beads or book) sin; breaking of bread or Lord's
> Supper sin, yea as odious as the oblation of Swine's
> blood, a Dog's neck or killing of a Man, Isa. 66.[33]

Williams was against forcing all to attend worship because he was against having the unregenerate persons pol-
luting the worship service and increasing their sinfulness. And having unregenerate persons in worship "hard-
ens up their souls in a dreadful sleep and dream of their
own blessed estate, and sends millions of souls to hell
in a secure expectation of a false salvation."[34] Williams
could not impose such higher standards for admission to
the Separatist and Puritan worship of churches he served
at Plymouth or Salem; but in his home at Providence, he
began worship admitting the regenerate only. He had
thought of the need for apostles to speak and convert
the unregenerate outside of worship; but not long after
his rebaptism at Providence, he discontinued personal
prospects to build any particular church group.[35]

Although the Providence First Baptist Church claims
Roger Williams as its first minister, the absence of
church records from that brief period frustrates assess-
ment of his worship order. But his writings express
ideas clearly animated in evidence of Providence's early
worship. Besides the exclusion of all but the regenerate,
there were other departures from the worship patterns
seen at Plymouth. While strongly affirming the need for
exhortation and questions in worship to try all teachings
with fire, he limited the speaking to men and insisted
women remain silent. We detail his views on that matter
in his critical discussion of Quaker worship later in
this chapter. His views against a hireling ministry were

reflected in the elimination of any offertory from worship at Providence.[36] But the absence of group singing through most of the seventeenth and eighteenth century worship at First Church Providence was not related to Roger Williams' views; for he chided the Quakers for "their monstrous way of Singing" but not for the act of singing in worship. The group singing and offering in worship were not noted as beginning in Providence's First Church until 1771.[37] Williams did not view the laying on of hands as essential for membership; and in the early years, First Church allowed such a practice but did not require it for membership until after 1654.[38] (Laying on hands was the distinguishing characteristic of six principle Baptist churches based on Hebrews 6:1-2).

Banished from the Bay Colony at the same period as Anne Hutchinson, John Clarke left Boston Puritan worship and led the development of worship at Newport where the First Baptist Church was formally organized in 1644. With the exception of requiring believers' baptism for participation, the Newport church worship resembled Boston church worship; and Clarke's new church did not follow the other departures noted at Providence. Group singing was included in worship from the beginning, although during the late seventeenth century it fell into disuse and was revived in 1726.[39] Laying on of hands for admission of members was not adopted as a requirement; and those favoring such a requirement withdrew in 1656 to form Second Church of Newport. Serving as pastor of Newport's First Church until his death in 1676 (except for an extended absence while representing Rhode Island interests in England from 1651 to 1663), Clarke carried his ideas to other communities in New England. We have only a partial view of Clarke's worship order for the service he led in 1651 at the home of a Newport church member who had moved to Lynn, Massachusetts. Clark was arrested for participating in that worship. Unfortunately, government witnesses did not enter until his sermon was in progress;

and they stopped the service before it had run its course.
Descriptions of that worship and other Baptist worship
of that period (protracted hymn singing, preaching, lay
exhortations, communion, etc.) are suggestive but not
fully documented.[40]   But from prison, Clark wrote the
court proposing a dispute of his principles with Bay
Colony ministers.   Although no such disputation was held,
Clarke spelled out his principles to the court.   The second and third principles bear directly on worship.   The
second required believer's baptism by immersion and allowed only such persons to participate in meeting house
worship.   The third urged lay prophesying as a duty in
worship:

> 2.   I testify that baptism, or dipping in water,
> is one of the commandments of the Lord Jesus
> Christ, and that a visible believer, or disciple
> of Christ Jesus (that is, one who manifesteth re-
> pentance towards God, and faith in Jesus Christ)
> is the only person to be baptized or dipped with
> water, and also that visible person that is to walk
> in that visible order of his house....
> 3.   I testify or witness, that every such believer
> in Christ Jesus, that waiteth for his appearing,
> may, in point of liberty, yea, ought, in point of
> duty, to improve that talent his Lord hath given
> him and in the congregation may ask for information
> to himself; or if he can, may speak by way of pro-
> phecy for the edification, exhortation, and comfort
> of the whole....[41]

Prosecution in 1665 of Thomas Goold and others (for
forming First Baptist Church in Boston) produced additional documentation of early American Baptist worship.
Goold, who served as pastor for the first decade, and
Thomas Osborne had been members in the 1640s and 1650s
at the Puritan church of Charlestown.   While Goold's
infant daughter was baptized there in 1641, he was admonished in 1655 for refusing to have another child baptized.   (Goold had become a close friend of Henry Dunster,
who served as president of Harvard College for fourteen
years but was forced to resign in October 1654 because of
strongly denying the validity of infant baptism: "All
instituted Gospel worship hath some express word of

Scripture, but Pedobaptism hath none."[42] He would not
remain silent about his views but had engaged two days
of public disputation on the matter in February of 1654).
Because of their views against infant baptism, several
admonitions were issued to Goold and Thomas Osborne between 1655 and July 30, 1665 when they were finally excommunicated for failure to appear at the Puritan worship and for persistence in holding their own worship
with the Lord's Supper.[43] And for persisting in such
worship, they were arrested and convicted by the civil
authorities.

Word of the worship and trial reached John Eliot
at Roxbury who made this entry in church records:

> July-August, 1665. The Anabaptists gathered
> themselves into a church, prophesied one by
> one, and some one among them administered the
> Lord's Supper after he was regularly excommun-
> icated by the church at Charlestown. They also
> set up a lecture at Drinkers house once a fort-
> night. They were admonished by the court....[44]

To the court, the Boston Baptist church leaders sent their
confession of faith. Parts of it relate directly to worship order: all were allowed to prophesy, for instance.
While the Providence Baptist Church had no covenant or
confession of faith, the following confession figured in
the worship life of the Boston Baptist Church from the
seventeenth through the nineteenth centuries:

> We believe with the heart & confess with the mouth
> that there is but (a) one god (b) Creator & governor
> of all things (c) distinguished into father, Son, &
> holy spirit (d) & that this is life eternal to know
> the only true god & Jesus Christ whom he hath sent
> (a) Deut. 6:4: I Tim. 2:5: Eph. 4:6: (b) Gen. 1:1:
> Hebs 11:3: (c) Matt. 8:16: I John 5:7: (d) John
> 17:3: Hebs 5:9: (e) & that the rule of this know-
> ledge faith & obedience concerning the worship &
> service of god & all other christian duties is the
> written word of god contained in the books of the
> old & new testaments (e) John 5:39: 2 Tim 3:15:16:
> 17: Deut: 4:2:5:6: Gen: 6:22: Exd: 20:4:5:6: & 39:
> 42:43: I Chron: 28:19: Psal: 119: Ezra: 8:19:20 &
> 27:13: Gall: 1:8: Rev 22:18:19: (f) we believe
> Christ is the foundation laid by the father (g)
> of whom Moses and the prophets wrote & the apostles
> preached (h) who is that great prophet whom we are

to hear in all things (i) who hath perfectly re-
vealed out of the bosom of his father the whole word
and will of god which his servants are to know believe and obey (f) Gen 3:14: & 22:13: (g) Deut:
18:15: Psal: 22:6:7:12: & 17 (h) Deut: 18:14: Acts
3:22:23: (i) John 1:18: & 12:29: & 15:15 & 17:18:
Matt: 17:5: 2 Tim: 3:15:16:17: (k) Christ his commission to his disciples is to teach & baptise (l)
And those that gladly received the word & are bap-
tised are saints by calling & fit matter for a visible church (m) And a competent number of such joined
together in covenant & fellowship of the gospel are
a Church of Christ (k) Matt: 28:19: Acts 9:10:18:
& 10:28: (l) Acts 2:41: (m) I Cor 1:1:2:4:5: Jer:
50:4:5: Psal: 50:5: Micha 4:5: Matt: 18:15:20 (o)
we believe that a church thus constituted are to
walk in all the appointments of Christ (p) And have
power from him to choose from among themselves their
own officers whom the gospel allows to administer
in the ordinances of Christ among them whom they
may depute or ordain to this end (o) Matt 28:20:
(p) Acts 14:23 & 6:3:5:6:Rom 12:4:8: Acts 9:10:18 &
10:47:48: (q) And this church hath power to receive
into there fellowship visible believers (r) & if
any prove scandalous obstinate & wicked to put forth
such from amongst them (s) when the church is met
together they may all prophesy one by one that all
may all learn & all may be comforted (t) & they
ought to meet together the first day of the week
to attend upon the Lord in all his holy ordinances
continuing in the Apostles doctrine & fellowship
& breaking bread & praise (q) Rom: 14:1 & 16:2:
(r) Matt 18:7: I Cor: 16:2: Acts 2:42: (v) we acknowledge majestracy to be an ordinance of god &
to submit ourselves to them in the lord not because
of wrath only but also for conscience sake Rom:
13:1:I Pet: 2:13:14 (w) thus we desire to give unto
god that which is gods & unto Caesar that which is
Caesar's & to every man that which belongth to them
(x) endeavoring always to have a clear conscience
void of offence towards god & towards men having
hope in god that the resurrection of the dead be
of the just unto life & of the unjust unto condemna-
tion everlasting (y) if any take this to be heresy
then do we with the apostles confess that after the
way which they call heresy we worship the father
of our Lord Jesus Christ believing all things that
are written in the law & in the prophets & in the
psalms (w) Matt: 22:21 (x) Acts 24:14:15:16: John
5:28 (y) 2 Tim: 1:13 & 3:14:15:16:17: Matt: 10:32.[45]

Prosecutions continued through the century and well
into the eighteenth century. Toleration (assured in the
1692 Charter and specifically legislated for Episcopalians
in 1727 and for Baptists in 1728) did not necessarily

apply even in the eighteenth century to those who tried
to leave Puritan churches to join Baptist churches.
Those in the Boston Baptist Church were repeatedly subject to civil charges for "Celebrating the Lord's Supper
by an excommunicate person" and administering the Lord's
Supper "to persons under censure of an Approved Church
among us."[46] And the Baptist Church at Boston celebrated
the Lord's Supper once a month from its founding through
the nineteenth century.[47] But constables arrested members of the congregation for Sunday worship at Goold's
home even when the Lord's Supper was not served. On
one of these occasions in 1669, the presence of children
in the worship as well as something of the worship order
were reported to the court. The worship had begun at
two o'clock in the afternoon with twelve adults and five
children present; and the following order of worship was
observed:

> When we came into the house, John Johnson was exhort-
> ing the people. After he had done, Thomas Goold
> spoke from that place in first of the canticles
> the second verse, let him kiss me with the kiss of
> his mouth, and then went to prayer and so ended.[48]

In church and court records referring to this and earlier
incidents, no mention was made of singing; but Goold's
account of differences with the Puritan churches reveals
no criticism of their singing in worship. So, Wood may
have been correct that exclusion of singing in early
Boston Baptist worship was an attempt to avoid attracting
attention to the illegal services.[49]

The Boston church baptized William Screven and later
licensed him to preach at Kittery, Maine from which he
had brought many others to be baptized in Boston. That
Kittery church drafted the first covenant to be used by
a Baptist church and resettled the following year in
Charleston, South Carolina to become the first Baptist
church in the South. The covenant is printed in full
as it was used in worship on the admission of new members.

> We whose names are here under written do solemnly
> and on good Consideration god Assisting us by his

> grace give up ourselves to the lord and to one an-
> other in Solemn Covenant, wherein we do Covenant
> and promise to walk with god and one with another
> in a due and faithful observance of all his most
> holy and blessed Commandments, Ordinances, Insti-
> tutions, or Appointments, Revealed to us in his
> sacred word of the old and new Testament and accord-
> ing to the grace of god and light at present through
> his grace given us, or hereafter he shall please
> to discover and make known to us through his holy
> Spirit according to the same blessed word all the
> Days of our lives and this will we do, If the lord
> graciously please to Assist us by his grace and
> Spirit and to give us Divine wisdom, strength, know-
> ledge, and understanding from Above to perform the
> same without which we can do nothing. John 15.4;
> Corinthians 3.5.[50]

Baptists immigrating into America from Europe rein-
forced the early patterns of lay prophesying and singing.
The transplanting of Welsh and Irish Baptist churches to
America and the arrival of Elias Keach (son of the English
Baptist champion of hymnody) did much to promote singing
among Baptists. Such strengthening of lay involvement
is noted in chapter four. The first church of Seventh
Day Baptists broke from Newport Baptist Church in 1671,
seven years after English Seventh Day Baptist Stephen
Mumford had joined Clarke's church; but their day of
worship was the only known departure from worship outlined earlier.

CONTINUING QUAKER WORSHIP IN AMERICA

Having seen the contours and sources of Puritan,
Separatist and Baptist worship in early America, one could
conclude that Quaker worship had a strong affinity with
the worship patterns of other free churches at the middle
of the seventeenth century. Historian Hugh Barbour may
have been correct that Quaker worship evolved from the
English Puritan mid-week prophesyings.[51] As noted earlier, such mid-week sessions also probably prepared Puritans
to accept Separatist worship order in America. But while
laity were given significant opportunity to speak out
during worship of all these seventeenth century churches

in America, how and why they spoke out made a major difference between the worship of Quakers and the worship
of the others. That difference was articulated by Roger
Williams who provided a haven for Quaker worship in Rhode
Island and recorded details about such worship although
he finally detested it. While more sympathetic accounts
of Quaker worship gave a general understanding of its
principles, critics (such as Williams) provided details
on its disquieting practice in early America.

The continuity between English Quaker worship and
subsequent American Quaker worship is clearer when one
realizes that quiet ways characterized eighteenth century
Quakers but not their seventeenth century progenitors.
From the records of seventeenth century London meetings,
Quaker historian Robert Barclay concluded "silence to
any large extent was the exception rather than the
rule."[52] The disruptive reputation of seventeenth century Quaker worship was spread by the holding of "thresh-
ing meetings" to win new converts to the Society of
Friends. Such meetings (filled with disruptions) were
a common form in colonies such as Rhode Island and Pennsylvania where the Quakers could legally worship.[53] And
the disruptive reputation was compounded in colonies
where Quakers could not legally worship and resorted to
outbursts in Puritan worship. For example, Judge Samuel
Sewall noted a number of disruptions such as the following in the worship of Boston's South Church on Sunday,
July 8, 1677:

> In Sermon time there came in a female Quaker,
> in a Canvas Frock, as her hair disheveled and
> loose like a Periwig, her face as black as ink,
> led by two other Quakers, and two others fol-
> lowed. It occasioned the greatest and the most
> amazing uproar that I ever saw.[54]

Quakers with less clothing made a witness in both England
and America that their leaders defended; but many leaders
of other free churches were appalled by travelling evange-
lists much less naked ones. In England, George Fox saw

such behavior as a type of non-verbal preaching:

> the Lord made one go naked among you, a figure of
> thy nakedness, and of your nakedness, and as a sign
> amongst you before your destruction cometh, that
> you might see that you were naked and not covered
> with truth.[55]

And in America, John Burnet and John Stubs called such
behavior a type of "testimony," but denied it was as common a practice in New England as Roger Williams inferred.[56]

In the Quakers' own meetings, set forms were eliminated so that the Spirit would be unquenched. In America
such elimination of forms went beyond excluding texts
for singing and nearly excluded the form of regular Sunday meeting itself. John Perrot's view that regular
Sunday meetings constituted a set form that could quench
the Spirit influenced Quakers from Virginia to Boston.
John Burnyeat's Journal reports that certain Friends in
Virginia during the last quarter of the seventeenth century had "quite forsaken their meetings, and did not
meet together once a year; and such sentiment had a
strong following in Boston as well.[57] George Fox's
trip to New England in 1672 was in part to counteract
the Perrot "heresy." Fox's "Advices," later developed
by the Books of Discipline, brought greater order into
Quaker worship life of the eighteenth century; but there
is a lack of evidence that Fox's "Advices" affected the
shape of American worship in the seventeenth century except that regular Sunday meetings survived. The absence
of detailed information on the meetings from Quakers
themselves forces one to rely on their critics or other
outsiders.[58]

In parts of eastern Pennsylvania and New Jersey,
there was a preference for worship meetings in the afternoon rather than in the morning.[59] Within the meetings
themselves, the injunction against set forms eliminated
texts for group singing; so, in the 1670s Roger Williams
witnessed spontaneous individual and unintelligible

group singing:

> their monstrous way of Singing and Toning and
> Humming many at once, as they often do and no-
> toriously did at Portsmouth on Rhode Island
> this last year, when no man is edified, nor
> understands what they say, and it may be not
> themselves (and this under color of singing
> in the Spirit) ....[60]

Williams went to the General Assembly of Quakers at Newport in 1671. At such Assemblies, Quakers from several
colonies came to conduct Society business and hold worship services on most of the days through the week. Attending one of the worship services, Williams reported:
"I queried with them about the true Christ, and the true
Spirit: but I was stopped by a sudden Spirit of Prayer
in a Woman, and the unseasonable Spirit of Prayer in a
man, which forced me to stop." And he noted that another
person burst into song and the assembly was dissolved
after a spontaneous prayer by another.[61]

To articulate fully his arguments with Quakers,
Williams arranged disputations with their leaders. In
these disputations, differences between Quaker worship
and other free church worship became evident. Quakers
believed that worship was not the place for questions
and arguments that could characterize Separatist, Puritan, and Baptist worship; but Williams believed that such
questions and disputes were essential to arrive at the
truth in worship:

> I told them, that they knew well, that the
> Spirit of God had given us abundant Warning
> against false Gods, false Worship, false
> Christs, false Spirits, false Prophets: He
> Commands us in Scripture not to believe them,
> etc. but to try them, to try all things, as
> we do with Touchstones, and with Balances,
> yea, with Fire itself.[62]

For Williams, "the true Prophets of God are willing to
have their Teachings questioned, examined and made clear
by the holy Records to the Souls and Consciences of all
men."[63] But the Quakers responded:

> the Spirit that gave forth Scripture is greater
> than the Scripture: the spirit is in us, that

> Spirit only opens the Scripture: the Spirit
> is immediate and infallible and they only who
> have this Spirit know the Scriptures.[64]

Williams agreed that the Spirit was needed in all acts
of worship including the opening of the Word; but he dis-
trusted their methods of allegorizing scripture.

Williams was especially critical of Quakers allowing
women to speak in public worship. He treated with con-
tempt their allegorizing of the women Paul ordered to
be silent. Williams allowed women to teach only their
children, other women, and their persecutors. Such a
view might justify Quaker women speaking out in Boston,
but certainly did not justify the Quaker women abusing
him in Providence as he recounted. But Quakers responded to such criticism with a text they did not need
to allegorize: "I will pour out my spirit upon all flesh,
and your sons and daughters shall prophesy."[65]

IV

CONTINUITY AND CHANGE OF WORSHIP ORDER

IN SEVENTEENTH, EIGHTEENTH, AND EARLY

NINETEENTH CENTURY FREE CHURCHES

Nearly two centuries of American free church developments occur between the seventeenth century worship patterns with strong lay participation and frequent communion (outlined in the first three chapters) and the nineteenth century ministerially dominated worship without communion. This chapter sketches some of those developments that invite many dissertations and other studies to reveal more distinctly the history of American free church worship. The development was not a gradual and continuous movement from frequent lay participation and communion to none. Frequent communion persisted in Congregational churches (as Separatist and Puritan churches came to be called); but the context of communion varied. In some areas, communion opportunities were constricted in winter months by severe winter weather coupled with increased distances between residences and churches; but communion opportunities were increased the rest of the year by growing numbers of churches and their celebration of the sacrament, increasingly called ordinance, on different Sundays of the month. While the Halfway Covenant created a large number of uncommunicating members in some churches, Solomon Stoddard opened the communion to these unregenerate as a means of converting them; but his grandson, Jonathan Edwards, urged followers to close communion to all except the regenerate. The immigration of other churches from Europe had diverse effects in free church worship. Presbyterianism influenced the increase of some Congregational ministers' authority at the expense of lay involvement; but

Methodism influenced the increase of lay participation
for a wide group of previously unchurched persons as well
as some former lay Anglicans who had had little say in
worship. While the lay role and frequent communion diminished in some churches, concern to revive just such
features of worship caused new churches to emerge: e.g.
Separatist and Baptist churches during the Great Awakening in the eighteenth century and the Disciples of Christ
during the Second Awakening in the nineteenth century.

CONTINUING AND CHANGING COMMUNION PATTERNS

AMONG CONGREGATIONAL CHURCHES

Writing at the end of the eighteenth century, Yale's
president Timothy Dwight observed that the Lord's Supper
"is customarily celebrated by a great part of the churches
in New England, on the first Sabbath of every month."[1]
There were both those who celebrated the Lord's Supper
less frequently and more frequently. He could not understand why Presbyterians celebrated it only twice or four
times a year. And in Boston, First Congregational Church
minister Charles Chauncy opposed those who argued for the
necessity of the Lord's Supper each Sunday. For him, a
monthly communion was normative.[2] In the seventeenth
century, his grandfather Charles Chauncy practiced weekly
communion as the Biblical norm. And that Chauncy was not
alone as John Winthrop observed:

> He did maintain, also, that the Lord's supper
> ought to be administered in the evening, and
> every Lord's day; and the church at Sandwich
> (where one Mr. Leveridge was minister) fell
> into the practice of it; but that being a mat-
> ter of no great ill consequence, save some
> outward inconvenience, there was little stir
> about it.[3]

After serving the Plymouth church and pastoring the Scitu-
ate church, the elder Chauncy served as President of Harvard from 1654 to 1672; but he was elected to that office
on the condition that he would not teach or publish his

views on the necessity of an evening Lord's Supper each
Sunday and baptism of infants by immersion. Even in the
early eighteenth century, celebration of the Lord's Supper at the end of the day was not unknown as witnessed
at Weymouth in 1705; but the norm among American Congregational churches through the first two centuries was a
Sunday morning communion once a month.[4]

"Inconvenience" had been noted by Winthrop as an
argument against evening communion each week; and in the
severe New England winters, even monthly morning communion
was difficult in some churches. Three times Samuel Sewall
noted in his diary that the communion bread was frozen
in winter celebrations of the Lord's Supper at Boston's
Old South Meeting House.[5] And eight other times, he notes
that the severity of the cold weather greatly diminished
the numbers at worship and particularly diminished the
number of women present.[6] Holding the Lord's Supper under such conditions was more than an inconvenience; for
absence from communion was an offense for which some
persons were chastised.

But the inconvenience varied from meeting house to
meeting house. Marian Card Donnelly notes:

> contrary to legend, the settlers did not invari-
> ably worship in unheated buildings. The contract
> for the enlargement of the meeting house at Salem,
> Mass., in 1638 specified "One Catted Chimney of
> 12 foote longe and 4 foote in height above the
> top of the building."[7]

And Salem Church records report communion the first Lord's
Day of each month without interruption.[8] But Plymouth
Church records reveal numerous occasions when communion
was postponed or not held during months of severe weather.
And the inconvenience of winter weather had increasing
effect. When Plymouth was served by settled ministers,
the church held monthly communion during most winter
months in the seventeenth century;[9] but in the first
quarter of the eighteenth century, communion was rarely
held in winter months and was even postponed once during
early October because of a violent storm.[10] The desire

for more frequent communion was evidenced as late as 1812 when the minutes of the January 6 meeting note,

> Agreeably to the request of some of the members, it was proposed for the consideration ... to omit the administration of the ordinance in the winter, & to have the communion more frequently in the milder seasons. But some of the members preferring the present arrangement, it was concluded to remain in usual practice....[11]

But the pattern of monthly celebration of communion among Congregationalists did not prevent members from participating in communion more often. Some churches celebrated the Lord's Supper on the first Sunday of each month while others celebrated it every four Sundays; and with the latter pattern, the communion was often on Sundays other than the first Sunday of the month. Samuel Sewall often participated in the Lord's Supper at other Boston churches or elsewhere in the same month he was enjoying the Lord's Supper at his own Old South Meeting House; for instance, he took the bread and wine at North Church on October 16, 1687 and at Old South on October 30, 1687.[12]

For Sewall, the Lord's Supper was the center of the Christian experience. Even before he joined Old South Church, he noted,

> Troubled that I could love Christ no more, it came into my mind that Christ had exhibited himself to be seen in the Sacrament, the Lord's Supper, and I conceived my want of Love was, that I could see Christ no more clearly.[13]

He reported relief in realizing that unworthiness was "an unwarrantable excuse that some make for not coming to the Sacrament...."[14] He wrote of his desire for the next Sacrament day; and his most moving accounts are occasioned by communion as in 1688:

> I sit down with the Church of Newbury at the Lord's Table. The Songs of the 5th of the Revelation were sung. I was ready to burst into tears at that word, bought with thy blood. Me thoughts 'twas strange that Christ should cheapen us; but that when the bargain came to be driven, he should consent rather to part with his blood, than goe without us; 'twas amazing.[15]

Abundant tears of joy were not unknown at the Lord's Supper during the seventeenth century. Increase Mather wept
happily and uncontrollably at communion.[16]

With love of the Lord's Supper, Sewall urged other
churches in Boston to celebrate the Supper every four
weeks in a staggered pattern so that no Sunday would
go by without the Sacrament being held in Boston.   In
his account of such urging on September 10, 1705, we
learn why First Church had departed from that custom:

> In the Afternoon I went to speak to Mr. Allen
> that the Lord's Supper might be celebrated once
> in four weeks, as it was in Mr. Cotton's Time
> and Mr. Wilson's: He was just come out of his
> house with Elder Bridgham, Elder Copp, Deacon
> Marion and Deacon Hubbard: I pray'd them to go
> back again, and open'd my mind to them. All save
> Mr. Hubbard plainly remember'd how it was in Mr.
> Wilson's days; and the Alteration upon the com-
> ing in of Mr. Davenport, upon his desire because
> he had it so at Newhaven: and seem'd inclinable
> enough to alter it. Then I went to Mr. Cooke,
> both he and Madam Cooke remember'd the change,
> and seem'd not displeas'd with my proposal. I
> discours'd with Mr. Pemberton, and told him it
> would be a Honor to Christ, and a great Privi-
> lege and Honor to Boston, to have the Lord's
> Supper administred in it every Lords Day: we
> having nothing to do with moneths now; Their
> Respect now ceases with the Mosaical Pedagogy.
> [Gal. iii. 24.] It seems odd, not to have this
> Sacrament administred but upon the first day of
> each Moneth; and the rest of the Sabbaths always
> stand by.[17]

But Sewall did not succeed in changing the pattern of
First Church as they continued celebrating the Lord's
Supper on the first Sunday of each month. And the Brattle
Square Church celebrated the Lord's Supper on the first
Sundays; and so, beginning in 1720, those two churches
held combined Friday lectures to prepare the people for
taking communion.[18] Sewall was more satisfied in 1714
when New North Church was organized and held communion
every four weeks in such a way as to supplement the communion patterns of the other churches. Having enjoyed
their communion on November 28, he returned for communion

on December 26 and noted:

> I did it to hold Communion with that Church;
> and, so far as in me lay, to put Respect upon
> that affronted despised Lord's Day. For the
> Church of England had the Lord's Supper yes-
> terday, the last day of the Week: but will
> not have it today, the day that the Lord has
> made....I did it also to Countenance a young
> small Church, and to shew that I was pleas'd
> with them for having the Lord's Supper once
> in four Weeks, and upon one of the Sabbaths
> that was vacant.[19]

The centrality of the Lord's Supper in New England's
spiritual life posed a problem; for present at worship
were both the church (persons with a regenerative experience that qualified them for church membership and communion) and the congregation (persons without a regenerative experience and unqualified for membership or communion even if they had been baptized.) As noted in
Chapter One, some churches celebrated communion after
dismissing the congregation; and other churches allowed
the congregation to witness the communion celebration
by the church. But there was always a hope that those
in the congregation would have the regenerative experience and so eventually partake of communion. The action
of the 1662 Synod (known as the Halfway Covenant) compounded this problem by allowing many more unregenerate
people to be baptized; for the ministers then faced a
larger proportion of baptized Christians unqualified for
communion. Different solutions to the problem were effected or attempted in different churches; and we need
numerous studies of the quite different efforts by Solomon Stoddard, Jonathan Edwards and his followers from
Samuel Hopkins to Nathaniel Emmons, and many others.
Communion continued to be celebrated once a month throughout the period of our study; but who was qualified to
take communion changed.

The wide spectrum of solutions is better understood
when one realizes that a number of churches either never
adopted the Halfway Covenant or repudiated it after a few
years. While the Wenham/Clemsford Church had been

practising a Halfway Covenant for six years before the
1662 Synod approved it, the Plymouth Church never adopted
that change.[20] First Church at Boston adopted the 1662
Synod action but then repudiated it in 1669. That church
readopted it in 1731 and did not again repudiate it until
1828.[21] While Solomon Stoddard approved the 1662 Synod
action, he and his Northampton Church were moving far
beyond it by 1677. We need studies on worship practices
in the church of each leading religious figure if we are
to know the precise history of free church worship; for
advocacy of changed forms may have come long after or
long before such changes were effected. Stoddard's numerous published works probably came long after he had
opened the Lord's Supper to the unregenerate at Northampton. Edwards' advocacy of restricting communion was a-
mong the reasons for his dismissal in 1750 before he
could effect the change; and Hopkin's dismissal in 1769
for a similar reason at Great Barrington further fore-
stalled implementation of Edwards' ideas. The significance of the Halfway Covenant in the seventeenth century
and Jonathan Edwards' ideas in the eighteenth century
may depreciate as historians give as much attention to
church record books as they have to theological books.
And such attention to church record books may lead to
an appreciation of Solomon Stoddard's significance; for
New England appears to have followed Stoddard far more
than Edwards.

With the publication of An Appeal To The Learned ...
Against the Exceptions of Mr. Mather in 1709, Solomon
Stoddard set forth most explicitly the changing qualifications for communion: "my position is, That Sanctifying Grace is not necessary to the lawful attending the
Ordinance of the Lord's Supper."[22] The "morally sincere"
person without regeneration was not only welcomed to communion but urged to participate. But Stoddard was tacitly
urging (and probably practising) such enlarged communion
thirty years earlier as witnessed by the wrath of Increase

Mather's 1677 Boston election sermon.[23] Stoddard as-
serted the equality of all worship much as Roger Williams
had done over a hundred years earlier as noted in Chapter Three; but Stoddard changed the qualification from
regeneration to propriety.

In 1709, he noted,

> many Persons do make an idol of the Lord's Sup-
> per; crying it up above all Ordinances both of
> the Old and New Testament, as if it were as pecu-
> liar to the Saints as heavenly glory.[24]

But nine years earlier, Stoddard had explicitly written
for the first time that even the unregenerate should take
communion:

> as no Man may neglect Prayer, or hearing the
> Word, because he cannot do it in Faith, so he
> may not neglect the Lord's Supper.[25]

And as early as 1687 he had urged all to attend diligently
all ordinances; for the Lord's Supper was "a special help
to those that are in the dark with a good conscience
...."[26] In The Doctrine of Instituted Churches published
in 1700, Stoddard noted that the Halfway Covenant had
kept people away from the sacrament of the Lord's Supper
and hardened some people's hearts from ever hoping for
regeneration. Even church members who thought themselves
regenerate and qualified for communion could not be certain they were numbered among the saints and eating and
drinking the Supper worthily unto blessing instead of
unworthily unto wrath; "and so Sacrament Days which should
be Days of Comfort, will become Days of Torment."[27] Increase Mather acknowledged the problem;[28] and Edward Taylor (who elaborated Mather's attack on Stoddard) argued
that the regenerate had the assurance of probable knowledge not just probable hope.[29] But Stoddard questioned
whether there was a biblical basis for requiring regeneration before communion: "They made no distinction ... into
communicants and non-communicants."[30] And he justified
his practice by scriptures likening the Lord's Supper to
the Passover which all could attend.[31]

While Stoddard opened the way for increased lay

participation in communion, he eliminated the need for
some other lay participation in worship: i.e. relation
of the person's regeneration experience. But even in
churches where the regeneration experience was required
for admission to church membership and the Lord's Supper,
the requirements for publicly relating that experience
diminished through the period of this study. Until 1756
in Boston's First Church, all men were required to relate
their spiritual experience in public worship before they
were admitted as members; but in that year it was voted
not only to eliminate the requirement for a relations
in worship but also to shift the consideration and vote
on admissions out of the worship to a time later in the
evening.[32] In 1730, there had been a motion to eliminate the public relation and substitute a private examination (satisfactory to the elders) followed by a public
confession of faith; but that motion was never acted
upon.[33] A private relating of regeneration was still
required until 1786 when the church followed the way
Stoddard had led over a hundred years earlier:

> Voted unanimously, that we remove every obstacle,
> which may prevent those who worship, from com-
> muning with us; and that we impose no other
> terms of communion than such as are found in
> the word of God or may be clearly inferred from
> it.
> Voted unanimously that all who believe in Jesus
> Christ, profess this belief, and sustain a good
> moral character, have a right to commune at the
> Lord's Table: it appearing from sacred author-
> ity, that nothing more was required of the primi-
> tive candidates for communion.[34]

Nothing more was required than that the person subscribe
to the Church's Declaration of Faith; and

> this may be done in private, provided the Church
> be informed that such candidate has made appli-
> cation ... and his actual subscription be an-
> nounced the first time he shall present himself
> to communion.[35]

In the Declaration of Faith, they promised "to watch over
each other as members of the same body."[36] But in 1843,
the minister proposed elimination of that promise; for

"it implies a closeness of relation that does not really exist [and] professes an oversight of one another that we do not admit."[37] By the next year, his proposal was approved and the Declaration of Faith shortened.[38] When subscription to even the shortened Declaration was offensive to some in 1856, the Church approved with but one dissenting vote "that our Pastor may feel authorized to admit any persons to our service of communion on their application and at his discretion."[39] And two years later, it was voted to give the minister discretion to hold the Lord's Supper after the benediction to the morning worship and "to invite all who desire to commemorate the love of the Lord Jesus to take part with us in the observance."[40]

The actions that transformed Boston's First Church from a strict Congregational church into a Unitarian one were mirrored in part by other churches who remained Congregational. But we need numerous studies of different churches in each region before we are able to generalize about the history of such changes in Congregational worship. For instance, Plymouth Church allowed one man to give his relations in private in 1677;[41] and eleven years later, a policy was established to allow men to give relations in private if the elders approved; "but those who could speak to hearing should soe doe in the whole congregation as formerly...."[42] In 1771, the Church rejected the argument that baptism alone entitled one to admission to the Lord's Supper.[43] Relations were still required for admission to membership and the Lord's Supper; but beginning in 1794, the relations were removed from worship and invited after the blessing.[44] In 1823, a Confession of Faith adopted in 1795 was rejected in favor of the original Church covenant. And in the same year, the Church reduced the form of the required relations:

> written relations as they are called, should no
> longer be required as a term of admission to
> Christian ordinances; but it should be optional

with the applicant to communicate his request
in writing or verbally through the Pastor.[45]
In 1829, the Plymouth Church eliminated voting on members
unless there was an objection to the person.[46] And finally in June 1837, the Church voted to make optional
even the simple public assent to the Church covenant:
the prospective member could profess it in private to
the pastor. As the First Boston Church had done, the
Plymouth Church took these actions "to remove from the
minds of sincere and devout persons every reasonable
objection against joining the Church and availing themselves of the satisfaction and benefit of enjoying the
Christian Ordinances."[47]

The First Church of Salem had eliminated the need
for relations as early as 1661, if the person applying
for admission had been baptized as a child before that
Church.[48] But not until 1771 did they eliminate the need
for relations by baptized adults moving into town from
other communities.[49] While oral relations were custom-
ary, one interesting exception was the admission of a
woman who could neither speak nor talk from birth. In
1730 she was examined and admitted to membership immediately before communion; and the pastor's propounding of
the covenant and her consent were entirely through sign
language.[50]

The persistent importance of the Lord's Supper in
Congregationalism to the end of this study in the 1830's
is illumined by its importance in the even more liberal
Unitarian churches that had split off from Congregationalism. On September 9, 1832, Ralph Waldo Emerson resigned
as minister of the Unitarians' Second Church in Boston
because that church would not approve changes in communion:

> As it is the prevailing opinion and feeling in
> our religious community, that it is an indispens-
> able part of the pastoral office to administer
> this ordinance, I am about to resign into your
> hands that office which you have confided to me.[51]

Three years earlier in a sermon on the Lord's Supper even

Emerson had extolled the virtues of communion in a way
reminiscent of Solomon Stoddard:

> the whole end and aim of this ordinance is but
> this, to make those who partake of it better.
> To join the church is not to say, I am good,
> or I have been, but I desire to be.[52]

INCREASING MINISTERIAL PREROGATIVES

FROM PRESBYTERIANISM IN CONGREGATIONAL CHURCHES

Among the seventeenth century Congregationalists
were numerous ministers and laity of Presbyterian persuasion. Presbyterians both inside and outside the Congregational churches influenced an increase of ministerial prerogatives at the expense of lay participation in
worship. The Presbyterian heritage did not lack precedents for frequent communion and lay speaking at meetings:
John Knox had advocated monthly communion at least; and
as late as 1711, the General Assembly urged Scotch Presbyterians to that more frequent celebration of the Supper.[53] And in Scotland, the pattern of "prophesyings"
or "interpretations" was imported from Geneva; so that
during the week in many late sixteenth century churches,
"every man had Liberty to utter and declare his mind and
knowledge to the Comfort and Consolation of the Kirk."[54]
But seventeenth and eighteenth century Presbyterians in
America do not appear to have followed those patterns
any better than many of their brethren in Scotland and
England where the prophesyings had been suppressed by
Queen Elizabeth and the Lord's Supper was commonly administered four times or less a year.[55] We need further
studies of particular churches where Presbyterianism
effected Congregational worship from the period of Presbyterian and Congregational cohabitation in some seventeenth century New England churches through the period
of their nineteenth century ecumenical cooperation starting mid-western churches under the 1801 Plan of Union.
The following instances may suggest the subjects of those

needed studies. And then we consider reasons besides Presbyterianism for the decline in lay speaking in Congregational worship.

Ministers of Presbyterian persuasion shaped some Puritan church worship in the Bay Colony from the 1630s. Rev. Peter Hobart served the Hingham church from 1635 through 1679; and Thomas Parker and James Noyes served the Newbury Church from 1635. These ministers tried (sometimes with strong lay objection) to minimize lay speaking in worship services and church business. Winthrop noted of Hobart:

> the pastor there, being of a Presbyterian spirit, did manage all affairs without the church's advice, which divers of the congregation not liking of, they were divided in two parts. Lieutenant Emes, etc., having complained to the magistrates, as is before expressed, Mr. Hobart, etc., would have cast him out of the church, pretending he had told a lie, whereupon they procured the elders to write to the church, and so did some of the magistrates also, whereupon they stayed proceedings against the lieutenant for a day or two.[56]

Hobart had clearly not reconciled himself to the results of the Cambridge Synod held in 1643. He had prompted that meeting to gain approval of his views including the idea that ministers should have the right to excommunicate church members without recourse to church vote. He held to the view that the laity should vote only on the calling of the minister. The minister then should have the right to admit and cast out members. Similarly, Thomas Parker and James Noyes at Newberry were lessening lay activity in the examination of candidates for membership by eliminating the requirement for a public statement of regeneration and admitting some who walked uprightly but may have lacked the regenerative experience. That Synod rejected Hobart's view on eliminating the church from admission and excommunication votes but opened the door to some of Parker and Noyes' practices on admission of members:

1. That the votes of the People are needful in all admissions and excommunications, at least in

> the way of consent; all yielding to act with
> consent - 2. That those that are fit matter
> for a church, though they are not always able
> to make large and particular relations of the
> work and doctrine of Faith, yet must not live
> in the commission of any known sin, or neglect
> of any known duty.[57]

While the majority of Bay Colony ministers did not
think they had opened the way for unregenerate to become
church members in 1643, Puritan ministers such as Thomas
Hooker in Connecticut were lessening lay requirements
to speak out in worship. In a book aimed to counter some
Presbyterian ideas expressed in Samuel Rutherford's The
Due Right of Presbyterians (1644), Hooker wrote in Survey
of the Summe of Church Discipline:

> Externally those are within the covenant, who
> expressing their repentance, with their profes-
> sion of the truth, engage themselves to walk in
> the ways of God, and in the truth of his worship,
> though they have not for the present that sound
> work of Faith in their hearts, and may be shall
> never have it wrought by God's spirit in them.[58]

Where the need to speak of regeneration was eliminated,
the need for other laity to speak out and question the
candidates in worship was reduced. The lessened rigor
of lay life was also reflected in the few instances of
church discipline carried out by Hooker's church: "There
was but one person admonished in, and but one person excommunicated from, the church of Hartford, in all the
fourteen years that Mr. Hooker lived there."[59] Many of
the Connecticut Congregational churches had elected lay
elders who were active in worship and led the prayers
in worship when the minister was absent;[60] but Connecticut also had ministers attempting to enlarge their powers.
John Davenport, whom Samuel Sewall had decried for changing the communion practices at Boston's First Church,
served earlier at the church of New Haven, Connecticut
where his efforts to minimize lay speaking in the examination of new members evoked an angry response from school-
master Ezekiel Cheever: members "have nothing to do now
but to say Amen, we are all Clerks now."[61] Davenport's

efforts led to his removal from first New Haven and then Boston.

The Connecticut General Assembly tried to impose the Presbyterian leaning 1708 Saybrook Platform on Congregational churches. Most of the churches in the eastern part of the colony rejected or minimized the implementation; but churches in the western part of the colony (nearer the Presbyterian influence in the middle colonies) elaborated the platform in an even more strongly Presbyterian direction.[62]

A hundred years later, the 1801 Plan of Union was another occasion of Presbyterian and Congregational collaboration. Working to minimize differences and effect a more ecumenical spirit and not necessarily to increase their own power, some ministers discouraged questioning by laity. Timothy Flint, whose Mississippi missionary activities had begun in the era of Congregational and Presbyterian cooperation, advised, "Disputation and discussion, under the mistaken idea of enlightening the understanding, tends to banish the small remains of religion among us."[63] And Flint continued, "But I have long been firmly of the opinion that the Catholics were right in representing much questioning and disputing of points as ruinous in their tendencies."[64] And one may easily understand how Presbyterian Lyman Beecher's responses would chill the questioning disposition of his hearers:

> A young man said to him, "What can I do if I am
> not elected?" "When you begin to care about be-
> ing saved, come to me and I will tell you; but
> while you don't care a snap about it, very likely
> God doesn't."[65]

And ministers of similar mind with Presbyterian Reuben Tinker would also discourage questioners:

> More objections might be stated, if not answered,
> for there is almost no end to the difficulties
> which occur to inquiring minds when they try,
> by the line of their reason, to measure the in-
> finitude of God. We cannot explain it. We need
> not answer half the questions that may be pro-
> posed.[66]

Having experienced anti-religious arguments of some En-
lightenment leaders, early nineteenth century religious
leaders were understandably less sanguine about the value
of questioning and discussing by laity.[67]

Ecumenical concern had also led some much earlier
Congregational ministers to present a minimal view of
lay speaking in worship. In writing his History of New
England from the Year 1620 to the Year 1680, pastor William Hubbard of Ipswich assured the reader that no one
besides the Plymouth Church allowed lay prophesying;[68]
but what the English reader understood as prophesying
was called exhorting and questioning in New England where
they were widely practiced in worship as we have recounted
in the first three chapters. But while some New Englanders took pains to present their churches as acceptable
to more established groups in England, the English Congregationalists had reaffirmed lay prophesying in the
1658 Savoy Declaration:

> Although it be incumbent on the Pastors and
> Teachers of the churches to be instant in
> Preaching of the Word, by way of Office; yet
> the work of Preaching the Word is not so pe-
> culiarly confine to them, but that others also
> gifted and fitted by the holy Ghost for it ...
> may publiquely, ordinarily and constantly per-
> form it."[69]

The Savoy Declaration and books of similar sentiment
equipped ministers such as John Norton to argue for lay
prophesying; and he became the minister at Hingham where
Peter Hobart's more Presbyterian views were rejected.[70]

At the end of the seventeenth century, the ecumenical concern for a rapprochement with the Anglican church
led some Puritans to form Brattle Street Church in Boston.
In November of 1699, they published their "manifesto" that
eliminated relations as a requirement for joining the
church and allowed such Anglican practices as the Lord's
prayer and uninterrupted reading of scripture in worship.[71]
There was strong negative reaction among some leading Puritans who believed the Brattle Manifesto was a betrayal of
the New England way.[72]

During the Great Awakening, there was a revival of lay speaking in Separatist and Baptist churches as we will explore in the next section of this chapter; but Charles Finney's assertion that Jonathan Edwards favored lay exhorting in worship is a distortion of fact. Edwards opposed lay exhortation, although lay leadership of prayer was allowable.[73] Edwards acknowledged that the Spirit might inspire laity to speak out in worship; but he urged them to restrain such an improper impulse; for such speaking was the ministers' function:

> I believe there may be a disposition in like manner indirectly excited in lay persons, through the intervention of their infirmity, to do what belongs to ministers only; yea, to do those things that would not become either ministers or people. Through the influence of the Spirit of God, together with want of discretion and some remaining corruption, women and children might feel themselves inclined to break forth and scream aloud to great congregations, warning and exhorting the whole multitude, and to go forth and halloo and scream in the streets, or to leave the families they belong to and go from house to house earnestly exhorting others; but yet it would by no means follow that it was their duty to do these things, or that they would not have a tendency to do ten times as much hurt as good.[74]

And he also opposed relations or any other form of lay speaking in public worship. Such speaking should be in private conversation.[75]

Toward the end of the eighteenth century, a number of Congregational ministers were exploring an alternative to lay speaking in public Sunday worship: they returned the lay speaking to mid-week meetings often held in the minister's home, although some ministers held such sessions between the two Sunday services. And other ministers refused to answer questions or channeled the questioner into a time of private conversation at a later time. Dr. Charles Backus, pastor at Somers, Connecticut from 1773 to 1803, held extra meetings in his home on both Wednesday and Sunday evenings. Training a number of young men for ministry, Backus provided them beforehand with questions on a scripture and opened the meeting

with five or six minute presentations by each student.
After his own application of the text, he invited any
lay person to propose questions.[76] At least one of his
students, Dr. Alvan Hyde, established a similar practice
at Lee, Massachusetts where he continued such meetings
throughout his pastorate from 1790 to 1833:

> He instituted weekly meetings in different parts
> of his parish, for the purposes of devotion and
> familiar exposition of the world of God; and,
> while he always took the lead in the exercise;
> he encouraged any who were present to make in-
> quiries, and even to state their views, concern-
> ing the portion of Scripture that occupied their
> attention.[77]

Dr. Josiah Catlin conducted a similar mid-week meeting
throughout his ministry from 1786 to 1826 at New Marl-
borough, Massachusetts; and Dr. John Brigham gave a more
detailed description of the order:

> In his weekly evening conference meeting, his
> usual method was, in connection with singing
> and prayers, to read a chapter in the Bible
> with a running exposition, and then to invite
> any disposed, to ask questions or to express
> their own views in regard to the chapter. It
> was surprising to see with what feeling and
> ability many of the members of his church would
> enter into these discussions, - men, too, of
> moderate education and daily toil.[78]

Further research is needed to discern whether Brigham,
Catlin, and Hyde derived their patterns from reading or
experience of earlier New England patterns.

    Lay speaking was discouraged either directly or
indirectly by some other ministers during the late eighteenth century. Ephraim Judson diverted the questions
away from worship and to another time and place:

> If any one wished to question him in respect
> to any thing contained in his sermon, as some-
> times happened, he always declined any contro-
> versy as unsuitable to the time, and invited
> the would-be disputant to call upon him, when
> he would converse with him as much as he might
> desire.[79]

Judson's practices were not popular; and he was dismissed
from his first two churches: serving from 1771 to 1778
at the Second Congregational Church of Norwich, Connecticut

and from 1780 to 1790 at Taunton, Massachusetts. He settled more agreeably with the church in Sheffield, Massachusetts from 1791 to 1813. Lay speaking was inhibited
by a much higher respect given Dr. Elijah Parish by his
church members from 1787 to 1825 at the Byfield Church
of Newbury, Massachusetts.[80] And a similar reason may
lie behind the experience of black minister Lemuel Haynes
who served parishes from 1785 to 1833 first in Rutland,
Vermont and later in New York. He opened the door to
discussions but had no response.[81] And one other reason
for a decline in lay speaking was caustically given by
Baptist minister Jacob Knapp observing a Rutland Hill
church:

> The Congregational brethren in this place were
> "old fogies." They would invite neither Finney
> nor Burchard to labor with them: nor did they
> get reconverted during this meeting. They did
> not believe in young converts speaking or pray-
> ing, for fear they might become proud.[82]

INCREASING LAY INVOLVEMENT AMONG SEPARATIST
AND BAPTIST CHURCHES IN THE GREAT AWAKENING

While lay speaking in worship was declining in many
Congregational churches through the eighteenth century,
Baptist churches were growing through encouraging such
lay speaking. Spirited renewals in churches during the
early 1740s benefitted in large measure these Baptist
churches and new Separatist Congregational churches that
would later become Baptist; for many of these churches
welcomed the outpouring of the Spirit by enthusiasts of
the Great Awakening. The Separatist Churches of the
1740s are not to be confused with those of a hundred
years earlier. New Separatist churches split off from
older Congregational and regular Baptist churches to
protest growing Presbyterianism in the Congregational
churches and to restore or increase such features of lay
activity in worship as lay prophesy, lay relations, and
frequent communion which they saw as warranted and

demanded by New Testament patterns. Much of this increase of lay involvement in worship among Baptist and
Separatist Congregational churches has been fully documented by C. C. Goen's definitive Revivalism and Separatism in New England, 1740-1800: Strict Congregationalists and Separate Baptists in the Great Awakening. There
is no need to recapitulate what Goen's has already thor-
oughly documented; but the following section supplements
Goen's study by way of some earlier and later materials.

Chapter Three has shown the beginnings of Baptist
worship in the seventeenth century when monthly communion
and lay speaking in worship were common. These patterns
were sustained as new immigrant groups arrived from England, Wales, and elsewhere where similar patterns were
in use. For instance, the following 1657 regulations
of worship at Ilston were representative of the Welsh
churches from which immigrants came:

> (1) The meeting at Ilston to begin every Lord's
> day at 8:00 in the morning....
> (2) To break bread at Ilston every month; and on
> that day, Brother Proud or Brother Jones to exer-
> cise the first hour; then an approved Brother to
> exercise in Welsh the next hour; after that a ser-
> mon to the World, then proceed to break bread, etc.
> (3) On other days, the first hour to be exercised
> in private by gifted brethren not yet sufficiently
> tried and approved, if business of hindrance hin-
> der not: the next hour to be exercised by approved
> prophets, or gifted brethren.[83]

Chapter Three noted that John Robinson developed his worship order with John Smythe whose ideas and followers
(such as Thomas Helwys) became influential in shaping
the English Baptist church; so, it is understandable
that the Robinson inspired patterns, that the earliest
American Baptists had adopted, were acceptable to Baptists immigrating from Europe later.

Lay speaking in worship was supported by the Philadelphia Association annual meetings of regular Baptist
churches after the Great Awakening began. The most extensive scriptural justification for laity to preach came
in 1746. Such justifications were used not only to allow

lay preaching but also to urge reluctant unordained persons to speak out:

> But such as will not exercise their gifts upon
> trial, or without ordination, or as gifted
> brethren, seem to come near to what the apostle
> speaks of, 1 Cor. xii. 15; "If the foot say,
> because I am not a hand, I am not of the body."[84]

In 1723, the same Association had been hesitant about lay
preaching; so, based on more local Baptist church records
before the Great Awakening, studies are needed to discern
fully the impact of the Awakening on increasing lay speaking.[85]

Also remaining to be seen fully (as Goen acknowledged) is the significance of the Separatist Baptist
spread in the South through the efforts begun by Shubal
Stearns, Daniel Marshall and others. In the 1750's these
New Englanders moved through Virginia and North Carolina
drawing together many Baptist churches committed to re-
storing New Testament practices such as weekly communion,
the holy kiss, love feasts, foot washing, and laying on
of hands.[86]

Both because of a continuing shortage of ministers
and because of a continuing commitment by some ministers
to lay involvement in the services they conducted, lay
speaking in Baptist churches continued beyond the end
of this study in the nineteenth century. Jacob Knapp,
whose ministry extended from 1822 to 1874, regularly
called for lay speaking in worship. But the focus of
such speaking was less like the prophesying or exhorting
in the early Puritan's morning worship; for it was more
like the relations given by laity in the early Puritan's
afternoon worship:

> Mr. Knapp, at the conclusion of the sermon, was
> accustomed to come down from the pulpit and ex-
> hort the impenitent to come to Christ, and con-
> verts to tell what God had done for their souls.[87]

But whereas relations would be spoken once only by any
one individual in a given Puritan church, relations could
be repeated again and again by the same individual in a
Baptist church. And limiting lay speaking to relations

tended to narrow the subject matter to the person's individual life rather than the larger social or political life that could be engaged by prophesying or exhorting.

In contrast, Hiram Stimson, whose ministry began in 1830, engaged lay speaking on a wider range of issues in his afternoon worship services:

> Instead of a sermon on Sunday afternoon, we
> often turned it into a conference talk, the
> meeting taking this turn naturally, and not
> by previous notice. Never advertise any such
> change, nor be afraid of taking the liberty
> of making it.[88]

But it is evident from Stimson's writing that such wider lay speaking in Sunday worship was far less common than the more limited lay speaking Knapp invited. There is evidence of similar limited speaking in Black churches.[89]

Laity did preach with regularity in Sunday worship of the nineteenth century when the church lacked a minister: e.g. deacon Lyman Hall at the Baptist church in Lottery Village, Rhode Island.[90] And even at the middle of the nineteenth century, Baptist laity were being urged to take the lead in the absence of ministers and speak out in Sunday worship as they did in mid-week conference meetings:

> Do not be satisfied with merely meeting for wor-
> ship when you have a minister present. This is
> idolizing the ministry, not honoring it. You
> gather together, not to meet the minister, but
> the Saviour. He has not said, When you come with
> a minister I am with you, but, Wherever two or
> three are met in my name, there am I in the midst
> of you. You can be profited as truly, if Christ
> be there, without a minister as with one.... Let
> some brother who, in your more private meetings
> has shown an adaptedness for this service, take
> the lead of the meeting. You can spend the time
> profitably in prayer, singing, reading the Scrip-
> tures, and exhortation. If every brother would,
> before the meeting, direct his attention prayer-
> fully to some passage of Scripture,& when you come
> together would give his brethren the result of
> his reflections, the service would not lack in-
> terest. If you prefer a sermon, any brother may
> be called upon to read one. President Davies'
> are the best that I remember for this purpose....
> I have said that your private meetings present

an opportunity for observing the gifts of the
several members of the church. The meeting on
the Sabbath, when no minister is with you, is
still better adapted to this purpose. Talent,
of any kind, always shows itself when there is
a demand for it. Give men an opportunity to
speak for God, let occasions arise in which men
feel that they are called upon to bear witness
for him, and lips will be opened which have long
been sealed in silence. You may thus find that
what you have been asking for from man, in vain,
God has sent you from among your own brethren.
Some brother whom you have wholly overlooked,
may be the very man whom God has chosen to minister to you in spiritual things.[91]

The advice to read another person's sermon in Sunday worship reminds us that the practices of nineteenth century
Baptists were a far remove from the way of seventeenth
century Puritans whose denunciations of reading sermons
we noted in Chapter One.

INCREASING LAY INVOLVEMENT AND COMMUNION AMONG METHODISTS

AND DISCIPLES OF CHRIST CHURCHES IN THE SECOND AWAKENING

Many leaders of Methodists in the eighteenth century
and the Disciples of Christ in the nineteenth century
were committed to weekly communion. But the Methodist
hierarchical governance prevented the realization of such
communion for most Methodists. In contrast, the Disciples' belief in priesthood of all believers and congregational polity allowed weekly communion that continues
to this day. Numerous questions remain unanswered until
we have more studies of actual worship practices in many
different Methodist and Disciples' churches to supplement
the excellent studies we now have of denominational policies and the practices of a few leading religious fig-
ures.[92]

John Wesley's own practice of worship in America was
within the Savannah, Georgia Anglican church during a
brief period in 1736 and 1737. The Sunday services included a communion in the main morning worship:

The English service lasted from five to half hour

> past six. The Italian (with a few Vaudois)
> began at nine. The second service for the
> English (including the Sermon and the Holy
> Communion) continued from half an hour past
> ten till about half an hour past twelve. The
> French service began at one. At two I cate-
> chised the children. About three began the
> English service. After this was ended I
> joined with as many as my largest room would
> hold in reading, prayer, and singing praise.
> And about six the service of the Germans be-
> gan: at which I was glad to be present, not
> as a teacher, but as a learner.[93]

While Wesley returned to England and continued to celebrate communion each Sunday within basic Anglican church
liturgical forms, the American Methodist societies were
later led by Francis Asbury who had passion for episcopacy
but little feeling for Lord's Supper.

Although remaining an Anglican, George Whitefield
prepared the way for a flexible Methodism in America as
he preached in a wide array of different settings. "Receive the sacrament constantly, nay, oftener than once
a month."[94] In the Great Awakening and until his 1770
death in America, George Whitefield urged more frequent
communion wherever available and called indifferent whatever theological or ceremonial obstructions might keep
a person away from communion in any churches around them.
In sermons, he even ridiculed such obstructions that
men such as Cotton Mather and Solomon Stoddard had taken
very seriously during their lifetimes a generation earlier:

> A good woman came to me some years ago, just as
> I had done preaching -- some people love to be
> impertinent -- what do you think, says she; of
> Cotton Mather and another minister? one said,
> I ought to receive the sacrament before my ex-
> perience was given in, the other said not, and
> I believe the angels were glad to carry them
> both to heaven. I said, good woman, I believe
> they have not talked about it since, for they
> will no more talk of these things.[95]

And he chided Methodists and Anglicans who insisted on
kneeling in communion and others who would never kneel:
"Kneeling and standing are indifferent, if the knee of

the soul be bent, and the heart upright towards God."[96]

With Wesley and Whitefield urging weekly communion,
it is understandable that lay leaders such as Robert
Strawbridge began to celebrate communion without ordained
elders in the 1760's.[97] Asbury later called Strawbridge's
Methodist society "the first society in Maryland -- and
America."[98] While Wesley urged Methodist society members
to attend Anglican communion services, the Methodist
church in America emerged around the time of a revolution
that made Anglican churches unacceptable and often un-
available to many Methodists. While Joseph Pilmore and
some others in urban areas followed Wesley's bidding,[99]
most American Methodists followed Wesley's advice on
communing at Anglican churches no further than they followed his advice on remaining loyal to the king during
the revolution. And as the Methodist church emerged in
America as a new church with few ordained elders, Methodist laity could receive authorized communion rarely.
Although some ordained elders showed concern to celebrate
weekly communion wherever they were, most Methodist societies were fortunate regularly to see a deacon or preacher much less an ordained elder.

Jesse Lee detailed one major 1779 effort in the upper
south to provide frequent communion for Methodists:

> Many of our travelling preachers in Virginia and
> North Carolina, seeing and feeling the want of
> the instituted means of grace among our societies;
> (and there being but few church ministers in that
> part of the country, and most part of them stran-
> gers to heart-felt religion) concluded, that if
> God had called them to preach, he had called them
> also to administer the ordinances of baptism and
> the Lord's Supper. They met together at the con-
> ference held at the Broken Back church this year,
> and after consulting together, the conference
> chose a committee for the purpose of ordaining
> ministers. The committee thus chosen, first
> ordained themselves, and then proceeded to or-
> dain and set apart other preachers for the same
> purpose, that they might administer the holy
> ordinances to the church of Christ. The preach-
> ers thus ordained, went forth preaching the
> gospel in their circuits as formerly, and ad-
> ministered the sacraments wherever they went,

> provided the people were willing to partake with
> them. Most part of our preachers in the south,
> fell in with this new plan; and as the leaders
> of the party were very zealous, and the greater
> part of them very pious men, the private members
> were influenced by them, and pretty generally
> fell in with their measures. However, some of
> the old Methodists would not commune with them;
> but steadily adhered to their former customs.[100]

On May 9, 1780, Asbury met with a number of the newly "ordained" ministers in Virginia and convinced them to stop
administering the Lord's Supper until the next year's annual meeting in Baltimore; so a schism could be avoided
and advice from John Wesley could be sought.[101] Of the
leading Methodist preachers who had been celebrating communion without official ordination in the south (e.g.
Philip Gatch, John Dickins, and James O'Kelly), only
O'Kelly was officially elected an elder (qualified to
serve communion) at the 1784 Baltimore annual meeting,
although Dickins was elected a deacon.[102] Wesley's later
letter conveyed to the 1784 meeting along with The Sunday
Service for the Methodists in North America, with other
occasional services, "advised the elders to administer
the Supper of the Lord on every Lord's Day."[103] Because
the Love Feast could be celebrated by deacons and preachers and Asbury was moved by it, the Love Feast became
better known than communion among many Methodists in late
eighteenth and early nineteenth century America.[104] And
the Love Feast was suited to the efforts of converting
others to the faith; for according to the 1773 action
at the first American Conference, "No person shall be
admitted more than once or twice to our Love-feasts or
society meetings without becoming a member."[105] At least
the Love Feast could be used on a limited basis with
those not yet church members. By the time local preachers were ordained in 1812, more than a generation of Methodists had grown up in a church where communion was infrequent. And although the 1812 action made the Love
Feast less necessary for Methodist churches, by that
time the Second Awakening was well underway; and churches

were reaching out to many unchurched Americans. In that
quest toward the unchurched, communion was little culti-
vated.

And in preparation for that evangelical quest, Wesley's 1784 order had been largely laid aside. His order
of worship had been a modest revision of the Anglican
service. In 1789 Asbury initiated a change of the service away from Anglicanism:

> The exercise of public worship on the Lord's
> day shall be singing, prayer and reading the
> Holy Scriptures, with exhortation or reading
> a sermon in the absence of a preacher; and the
> officiating person shall be appointed by the
> elder, deacon, or traveling preacher for the
> time being.[106]

It was that Asbury initiated order of worship that increasingly characterized the recommended Methodist church
worship. In the Doctrines and Discipline, the public
worship was directed as follows:

> 1. Let the morning service consist of singing,
> prayer, the reading of a chapter out of the
> Old Testament, and another out of the New, and
> preaching.
> 2. Let the afternoon service consist of singing,
> prayer, the reading of one chapter out of the
> Bible, and preaching.
> 3. Let the evening service consist of singing,
> prayer, and preaching.
> 4. But on the days of administering the Lord's
> Supper, the last two chapters in the morning
> service may be omitted.[107]

But toward the end of the period in this study, even that
simplified order was not uniformly observed as evidenced
by a committee report at the 1832 Conference:

> The reading of the Scriptures in the morning
> and afternoon services, and the public use
> of the Lord's Prayer is generally practised,
> though not as uniformly as can be wished, and
> in some instances the sacraments are adminis-
> tered without using our prescribed and excel-
> lent forms; but in these things there has been [108]
> an evident improvement in the last four years....

Communion, although celebrated infrequently in many
Methodist churches in the nineteenth century, continued
to be characterized by wine. Grape juice was not

required in place of wine until the actions at the 1876
Conference. And there were leading Methodists with caus-
tic words for those who tried to effect such a change.
In Boston, Edward Taylor's support of the temperance
movement fell short of placing grape juice (which he
dubbed "raisin water") on the Lord's Table. In last
instructions to his church before he died in 1871, he
advised, "Cast from this church any man that comes up
to the altar with his glue pot and his dye stuff."[109]

In black churches, the order of Sunday morning worship was similar to white worship; but there were differences both in the ceremonial ways of doing the order and
in the meaning of what was said and sung, especially in
the south. The "ring shout" and other religious dance
incorporated what are now recognized as elements of west
coast African "high life" steps and facilitated a respon-
sive pattern of preaching and teaching; and the words in
spirituals became codes to express not only antagonism
to salvery but also hopes and plans to escape to freedom.[110] Lay speaking was frequent; but communion was not
central.

In the late eighteenth century, blacks accounted for
up to twenty-five percent of the membership in Methodist
and Baptist churches; and blacks were in many instances
noted as lay exhorters both officially and unofficially.
Albert Raboteau's definitive study, Slave Religion: The
"Invisible Institution" in the Antebellum South, detailed
instances of lay black exhorting in Baptist worship as
early as 1766 and discusses leading black exhorters in
Baptist and Methodist churches after the Revolutionary
War. The first separate black Baptist church was founded
between 1773 and 1775 at Silver Bluff in South Carolina
and encouraged blacks who later founded and led other
black churches outside the country.[111]

Because only ordained elders could serve communion
in the Methodist Church and because southern laws precluded blacks from being elected to such positions that

required freedom of movement, communion was possible only
at times when whites were leading worship. And so, in
the south where black membership was the largest, communion was disassociated from black leadership. And in the
north, Richard Allen did not found the first black Methodist church until 1787 in Philadelphia; and it was not
until 1816 that the African Methodist Episcopal Church
was organized as a new denomination and he was elected
bishop.

Another reason for the disassociation of Sunday communion from black worship was that the central black worship experience was in clandestine evening services
through much of the south during the first half of the
nineteenth century. At such worship services, lay speaking abounded: "Truly communal, these meetings, as Hannah
Lowery noted, needed no preacher because 'everyone was
so anxious to have a word to say that a preacher did not
have a chance. All of them would sing and pray.'"[112]
Black aspirations were expressed through these evening
services (where many lay persons could speak out in witness and prayer) rather than through Sunday morning services (where the most pressing concerns could not be communicated openly.)

Another new denomination born in the early nineteenth
century made weekly communion the center of Sunday worship. The Disciples of Christ or Christian Church did
not have the hierarchical problems that deterred Methodists from developing weekly communion. Although the
leaders of this new movement called for a return to the
"ancient order of things" with the New Testament as the
model for worship conduct, a thorough study is needed to
discern their more immediate antecedents. Primarily
based on readings of the New Testament, the Disciples'
Sunday worship appears remarkably similar to the patterns
developed two hundred years earlier by Separatists and
Puritans whosedevelopment of worship was similarly guided
by reading the New Testament. The important difference

between the new Disciples' pattern and the earlier Separatist and Puritan pattern was that Disciples' laity could lead the weekly communion with or without a minister present; for the priesthood of all believers was basic for the Disciples' practice.

The primary leaders, Barton Stone and Thomas and Alexander Campbell, came out of the Presbyterian Church where before we have seen calls for more frequent communion not generally practised. And their ideas and practices have been attributed to the Scottish followers of John Glas and Robert Sandemann whose eighteenth and nineteenth century churches in Scotland, England, and America practised weekly communion based on a priesthood of believers and congregational polity.[113] Stone was at the center of the 1801 "Cane Ridge" Kentucky revivals that is commonly seen as the beginning of the Second Awakening in the upper south; but communion did not figure in a major way in those revivals or in many later camp meetings that were concerned primarily in converting the unchurched.[114] And it is unclear how early Stone began practising weekly communion. Stone and others in the Springfield Presbytery formed the Christian Church in 1804. Some followers of Stone wrote more about actual worship services than he did; and from such accounts we learn that "the old fashioned exercise of shaking hands" figured prominently in the worship along with weekly communion.[115] But Campbell would note that passing of the peace was not essential.[116]

Alexander Campbell wrote profusely about both worship policies and practices. Along with his father Thomas Campbell, who was a Presbyterian minister in western Pennsylvania, Alexander Campbell appears to have been practising weekly communion at least as early as 1811 or 1812 when both Campbells had come to a firm belief in the centrality of communion in Christian worship:

> instituted worship can be nowhere performed upon
> the Lord's day, where the Lord's Supper is not
> administered. Wherever this is neglected, there

New Testament worship ceases.[117]
In 1813, Alexander left the Presbyterian Church to con-
nect his new Disciples' following with the Baptists. Although they had baptism by immersion in common, the Disciples' connection with the Baptists was an uneasy one;
for many Baptist churches celebrated the Lord's Supper
only once a month (and a few did it but once every three
months). And Campbell did not believe in requiring prospective members to give "relations" before admission.
For these and other reasons, he led followers out of
the Baptist connection and into a union with Stone's
Christians in 1832.[118]

In The Christian System in Reference To The Union of
Christians and Restoration of Primitive Christianity As
Plead By The Current Reformation, Alexander Campbell provided an extensive discussion of both his recommended
principles and practices of worship. And through the
pages of the Christian Baptist and later the Millenial
Harbinger periodicals, he addressed numerous questions
on the order and conduct of worship. While favoring lay
speaking in worship, he advised it be done in an orderly
fashion. Many churches such as the one at Pittsburgh,
Pennsylvania and the one at Cross Roads, Virginia were
practising exhortations in worship where every member
was urged to prophesy; and so, Samuel Rogers was prompted
to ask, "What, my brethren, is the church to be a
mouth?"[119] But Campbell highly recommended orderly lay
speaking and included it along with a great deal more
in his description of the ideal worship he recounted.
That description is a fitting close to this chapter as
it was to his chapter on "Breaking the Loaf":

> The following extract from my memorandum-book
> furnishes the highest approach to the model
> which we have in our eye of good order and
> Christian decency in celebrating this insti-
> tution. Indeed, the whole order of that con-
> gregation was comely:
>
> "The church in _____ consisted of about
> fifty members. Not having any person whom

they regarded as filling Paul's outlines of a bishop, they had appointed two senior members, of a
very grave deportment, to preside in their meetings.
These persons were not competent to labor in the
word and teaching; but they were qualified to rule
well, and to preside with Christian dignity. One
of them presided at each meeting. After they had
assembled in the morning, which was at eleven
o'clock, (for they had agreed to meet at eleven
and to adjourn at two o'clock during the winter
season,) and after they had saluted one another
in a very familiar and cordial manner, as brethren
are wont to do who meet for social purposes; the
president for the day arose and said, 'Brethren,
being assembled in the name and by the authority
of our Lord and Saviour Jesus Christ, on this day
of his resurrection, let us unite in celebrating
his praise.' He then repeated the following stanza:

> 'Christ the Lord is risen to-day!
> Sons of men and angels say;
> Raise your joys and triumphs high,
> Sing, O Heavens! and, earth, reply.'

The congregation arose and sang this psalm in ani-
mating strains. He then called upon a brother,
who was a very distinct and emphatic reader, to
read a section of the evangelical history. He
arose and read, in a very audible voice, the history of the crucifixion of the Messiah. After a
pause of a few moments, the president called upon
a brother to pray in the name of the congregation.
His prayer abounded in thanksgivings to the Father
of Mercies, and with supplications for such blessings on themselves and for all men as were promised
to those who ask, or for which men were commanded
to pray. The language was very appropriate: no
unmeaning repetitions, no labor or words, no effort
to say any thing and every thing that came into his
mind; but to express slowly, distinctly, and empha-
tically, the desires of the heart. The prayer was
comparatively short; and the whole congregation,
brethren and sisters, pronounced aloud the final
Amen.

After prayer a passage in one of the Epistles was
read by the president himself, and a song was called
for. A brother arose, and after naming the page,
repeated:

> 'T'was on that night when doom'd to know
> The eager rage of every foe; --
> That night in which he was betrayed, --
> The Saviour of the world took bread.'

He then sat down, and the congregation sang with

much feeling.

I observed that the table was furnished before the
disciples met in the morning, and that the disciples
occupied a few benches on each side of it, while
the strangers sat off on seats more remote. The
president arose and said that our Lord had a table
for his friends, and that he invited his disciples
to sup with him. 'In memory of his death, this
monumental table,' said he, 'was instituted; and
as the Lord ever lives in heaven, so he ever lives
in the hearts of his people. As the first disciples, taught by the Apostles in person, came together into one place to eat the Lord's supper,
and as they selected the first day of the week in
honor of his resurrection, for this purpose; so we,
having the same Lord, the same faith, the same hope
with them, have vowed to do as they did. We owe
as much to the Lord as they; and ought to love,
honor, and obey him as much as they.' Thus having
spoken, he took a small loaf from the table, and
in one or two periods gave thanks for. After thanksgiving, he raised it in his hand, and significantly
brake it, and handed it to the disciples on each
side of him, who passed the broken loaf from one
to another, until they all partook of it. There
was no stiffness, no formality, no pageantry; all
was easy, familiar, solemn, cheerful. He then took
the cup in a similar manner, and returned thanks
for it, and handed it to the disciple sitting next
to him, who passed it round; each one waiting upon
his brother, until all were served. The thanksgiving before the breaking of the loaf, and the
distributing of the cup, were as brief and pertin-
ent to the occasion, as the thanks usually presented
at a common table for the ordinary blessings of
God's bounty. They then arose, and with one consent
sang, --

> 'To him that loved the sons of men,
>   And wash'd us in his blood;
> To royal honors raised our heads,
>   And made us priests to God!'

The president of the meeting called upon a brother
to remember the poor, and those ignorant of the way
of life, before the Lord. He kneeled down, and the
brethern all united with him in supplicating the
Father of Mercies in behalf of all the sons and
daughters of affliction, the poor and the destitute,
and in behalf of the conversion of the world. After
this prayer the fellowship or contribution was attended to; and the whole church proved the sincer-
ity of their desires, by the cheerfulness and lib-
erality which they seemed to evince, in putting
into the treasury as the Lord had prospered them.

A general invitation was tendered to all the brotherhood if they had any thing to propose or inquire, tending to the edification of the body. Several brethren arose in succession, and read several passages in the Old and New Testaments, relative to some matters which had been subjects of former investigation and inquiry. Sundry remarks were made; and after singing several spiritual songs selected by the brethren, the president, on motion of a brother who signified that the hour of adjournment had arrived, concluded the meeting by pronouncing the apostolic benediction.

I understand that all these items were attended to in all their meetings; yet the order of attendance was not invariably the same. On all the occasions on which I was present with them, no person arose to speak without invitation, or without asking permission of the president, and no person finally left the meeting before the hour of adjournment, without special leave. Nothing appeared to be done in a formal or ceremonious manner. Every thing exhibited the power of godliness as well as the form; and no person could attend to all that passed without being edified and convinced that the Spirit of God was there. The joy, the affection, and the reverence which appeared in this little assembly was the strongest argument in favor of their order, and the best comment on the excellency of the Christian institution."[120]

V

CHANGING BIBLICAL IMAGERY AND AMERICAN IDENTITY

IN SEVENTEENTH AND EIGHTEENTH CENTURY SERMONS AND ARTS

Changing patterns of Biblical texts and images chosen and developed by leading Puritan preachers in sermons
reveal changing American identity and theology in the
seventeenth and eighteenth centuries; and those changes
correspond to some of the changing worship patterns
noted in the previous chapter. For instance, set against
contrasting patterns in Puritan preaching of old England,
John Cotton concentrated on the Pentateuch and former
prophets, the Mathers shifted to the Wisdom literature,
and Edwards shifted to the Gospels. Corresponding
shifts may be noted in the conceptions of covenant:
e.g. a covenant with the people, a covenant with a remnant, and a covenant with the individual or no societal
covenant. Awareness of these shifts in imagery and
identity aids not only the theologian and church historian but also the art historian; for parallel shifts
my be discerned in the imagery of music and visual art
in and out of worship settings.

The period of New England sermons in this chapter
extends from the founding of the Bay Colony in the 1630's
until the beginning of the American Revolution in the
1770's. Most sermons after that period and well into
the nineteenth century offer little Biblical exegesis
or exposition. More scholarly sermons of the early
nineteenth century eschewed Biblical exegesis in a preoccupation with theological battles. Some preferred
exegesis of Edwards over exegesis of the Bible: as New
Testament scholar Calvin Stowe noted, "The prime cause
of this degeneracy lay in the fascination and success
of Edward's metaphysical writings."[1] And more popular
sermons of the nineteenth century were preoccupied with

converting individuals; and the preachers of such sermons
demonstrated depth knowledge of the cultural idolatries
that competed for the audience's allegiance but little
knowledge of Old and New Testament texts. The lack of
academic training may be seen as accounting for the
absence of biblical preaching among ministers in newer
denominations; but the theological preoccupations of
the day (not unrelated to concern for revivals) eliminated attention to Biblical exegesis even among most
well educated nineteenth century American preachers.
Edward Taylor's biting comment on one man's sermon char-
acterizes the era: "My dear brother, if your text had
the smallpox, your sermon never would have caught it."[2]
An exception to the foregoing pattern was the continued
vitality of preaching among black Christians firmly
based on the book of Exodus.[3]

To illumine the changing patterns in the seventeenth
and eighteenth centuries, a survery was made of the use
of biblical quotations or allusions in some twenty sermons, half preached in England between 1590 and 1663, the
other half preached in New England between 1634 and 1773.
The preachers, their sermons, and the type and number of
quotations from the Old and New Testaments and locations
in Evan's "American Imprints" are given in the table at
the end of this chapter. The number of sermons examined
here is small; but a wider preliminary survey of additional sermons show the sermons are fairly representative.
Quotations and allusions from the Bible are classified
into five types of Old Testament passages and seven types
of New Testament passages. The passages are not classified merely by the biblical book from which they come,
but by the kind of content which the preacher found in
them.

The first classification, "OT Narrative: People of
God," includes narrative passages from the Pentateuch,
the historical books and the Psalms, and occasionally
the prophets. "OT Prophecy" includes passages treated

as prophecy from the prophetic books, the Psalms, Deu-
teronomy, and the Deuteronomic history. "OT Wisdom"
passages are didactic, mostly from Proverbs, Job, and
Ecclesiastes. "OT Psalms of Individual Lament" and "OT
Corporate Worship" are obvious categories.

"NT Quotation or Allusion to OT" passages are those
which could just as well have been taken from the OT.
For example John Cotton used Matthew 12:42 "The Queen
of the South ... came ... to hear the wisdom of Solomon"
as a convenient summary of 1 Kings 10:1-10 or 2 Chronicles
9:1-12 to justify traveling to gain knowledge. Taking
these quotes into consideration we find a greater favor
toward the Old Testament in some sermons than totals
show. "NT Narrative of the People of God" passages concern some episode in the sacred history of the New Testament people. Many of these are taken from Acts, some
from Paul. "NT Teaching (Parables, Exhortations, etc.)"
includes the New Testament equivalent of both prophecy
and wisdom literature. "NT Individual as Example" are
quotations drawing on the examples of persons such as
Paul or Apollos for edification. "NT Abstract Theology"
are references to the pre-existent Christ in the pro-
logue of John, the doctrine of atonement in Hebrews, and
the doctrine of depravity in Paul. "Christ as Example:
the Nature of Leadership; Our Commission" are three interrelated themes that come together especially in the sermons of Jonathan Edwards.

The letter "T" in the tables marks the text on which
the sermon is based, if any is given. A number in parentheses indicates the number of quotes that grossly mis-
apply the idea of the Biblical passage in terms of the
theological understanding of that time, or that challenge
it. These numbers are quite small. The Bible was usually
made to fit the interests of changing times by quoting
from different parts rather than by quoting out of context.

The English conservatives whose sermons are sampled
include Richard Hooker (1554-1600), Lancelot Andrewes

(1555-1626), and William Laud (1573-1645). Hooker wrote
Laws of Ecclesiastical Polity in 1593, which laid the
foundation for the conservative position. Andrewes was
chaplain to Elizabeth and James, was Bishop of Winchester,
and dean of English preachers, and was considered a man
of great spiritual depth. Laud as chief advisor to
Charles I (and Archbishop of Canterbury) was narrow but
sincere, imitating Andrewes' spirituality. He was exe-
cuted by the revolutionary government in 1645.

The English Puritans sampled are Thomas Cartwright
(1535-1603), William Perkins (1558-1602), William Ames
(1576-1633), and John Cotton (1584-1652), who is also
part of the American sample. Cartwright was deprived
of his professorship in divinity at Cambridge for non-
conformist views. Perkins was a fellow of Christ's
Church Cambridge, a renowned preacher and writer, and
a leader of the dissenting movement. Ames codified
dissenting thought and influenced Cotton and other New
England leaders. In England, Cotton was vicar of St.
Botolph's in Boston, Lincolnshire, for twenty years,
enjoying a reputation as preacher and theologian. When
forced to resign in 1633 for non-conformity, he went to
New England and became Teacher of the Boston church where
he developed the worship patterns discussed in the first
two chapters.

The New England Puritans sampled are, in addition
to Cotton, Samuel Willard (1640-1707), Increase Mather
(1639-1723), Jonathan Edwards (1703-1758), Samuel Hopkins
(1721-1803), Nathanael Emmons (1745-1840), Charles
Chauncy (1705-1787), and Jonathan Mayhew (1720-1766).
They were all leading New England preachers in their
respective times.

A glance at the tables shows that the three English
conservatives all quote more from the Old Testament than
from the New. Most of the Old Testament quotations are
from the Narrative and Prophetic classifications. The
New Testament quotations are from Narratives of the People

of God, and Teaching; and in the case of Andrewes, from the Abstract Theology classification. The overall emphasis is on the proper functioning of the individual in the corporate society.

In contrast, the four English Puritans all quote overall more from the New Testament than the Old. (The four "addresses" by Ames are very short, and have been averaged.)[4] Almost all the quotations from the New Testament are from the category of Teaching, except with Perkins, for whom has been substituted the treatise A Discourse on Conscience, which also includes many New Testament quotations from the Abstract Theology category.[5] The overall emphasis among the English Puritans is on the salvation and sanctification of the individual.

The early American preachers, however, show a marked difference from their fellow Puritans in England. John Cotton's English sermon favors the New Testament 25 to 14, whereas his New England sermon God's Promise to his Plantations favors the Old Testament 47 to 13. The first two or three generations in New England preached largely from the Old Testament and emphasized the corporate community.

UNDERSTANDING IMAGERY OF THE PENTATEUCH

AND COVENANT WITH THE PEOPLE

Cotton's New England sermon God's Promise to his Plantations takes its text from and centers its argument in the epic of God establishing the nation Israel in Palestine, and the prophets' exhortations to Israel to maintain its relation with God. The parallel with the establishing of New England is clear. This sermon, delivered within five years of the arrival of the Puritans in Massachusetts, makes some effort to justify the project, but also suggests that the experiment was already beginning to justify itself by its own success -- preacher and congregation sensed the solid achievement of a good start at creating a new community in the face of great

danger, by reliance on God and the willingness of every
individual to share responsibility for the community.
And they saw the analogy with the creation by the people
of Israel of that other new community described in the
Bible.[6]

Samuel Willard's A Sermon Preached on Ezekiel, 45
years later, preserves the same point of view. The view
is more confident; gone is any attempt to justify the
colony. There is more explicit reference to the responsibility of individuals toward the community. The slight
shift toward Old Testament Prophecy over Old Testament
Narrative may correspond to the emergence of telltale
signs of the end of the great experiment in individual
responsibility to the group. The sermon complains about
the more recent loss of responsibility. Similarly the
golden age of Israel's tribal confederacy had produced
the great narrative epics; and the rise of a self-centered
commercial and ruling class under the monarchy had brought
on the prophets, who complained that things were not as
good as they used to be. With the rapid increase of population in New England and the loss of relative political
isolation from England, the New Englanders saw their experiment go through stages in 60 years that took 600 years
in ancient Israel.[7]

There is a very evident similarity between this
sermon of Willard's, A Sermon Preached on Ezekiel ...
Occasioned by the Death of John Leverett, Governor of
Massachusetts, and William Laud's sermon "To King James
on the King's Birthday," one of the Laudian sermons analysed in the tables. There are differences between the
two sermons, of course. Laud's sermon is much more faun-
ing, making an analogy with the Davidic covenant, which
is more flattering, rather than the Mosaic covenant as
Willard does. After all, the King had more power over
his chaplain than the Governor did over a New England
preacher; and besides, the King was sitting there listening, whereas Leverett was safely in a coffin. But the

overall point, the analogy between the state and ancient
Israel, was the same. In both sermons, state and church
were complementary ways of organizing the people of God
to enable them to live under God's sovereignty.[8]

UNDERSTANDING IMAGERY OF THE WISDOM LITERATURE

AND COVENANT WITH A REMNANT

But within the time of Willard, the preeminent place
of the analogy of the colony with Israel began to be con-
tested by another view. Was the New Israel in New England
the whole colony or just the regenerate members of local
churches? Was God's covenant with New England or with
the local congregation? In past practice, the church
members, who had the vote, acted as leaders responsible
for the whole colony; but one part of Puritan theory,
with Calvin's individual salvation predestined on a one
by one basis, did not support this practice. In an earlier period, consistent individualists like Anne Hutchinson
and Roger Williams were expelled for the sake of the community's survival. But by Willard's time, Massachusetts
was beginning to be able to afford the luxury of a little
individual self-centeredness.

This theological confusion shows up in a comparison
of Willard's two sermons, A Sermon Preached on Ezekiel
and The Duty of a People, both analysed in the tables.
They were preached at about the same time, but the first
was "Occasioned by the death of John Leverett, Governor
of Massachusetts", while the second was preached after
the Second Church in Boston "had explicitly and most
solemnly renewed the engagement of themselves to God
and to one another." The first drew an analogy between
the old Israel and Massachusetts; the second attempted
an analogy between Israel and Second Church. The first
had 64 references to the Old Testament, the second only
15. The first made a satisfying analogy between the two
communities in general and their various worthy leaders

in particular, including Governor Leverett; but the second, starting off well enough with the solemn choice by the people of Israel to follow God in Joshua 24, is then reduced to a description of the effect of this choice on the individual rather than on the community, thus doing violence to the literal meaning of several Bible texts quoted. Then Willard quotes from Psalms of individual lament and ends with prayer that God " ... strengthen you with all might in the inner man ..."[9]

The Increase Mather sermon "Birth Sin" in the tables is a very late sermon for Mather and comes forty years after the Willard sermons. By this time, the ambiguity of Willard's time has disappeared. In this sermon, the relation of the colony to Israel has disappeared and the trend is toward individualism and the use of Old Testament Wisdom and Psalms of individual lament together with a large number of quotations from the doctrinal parts of the New Testament to show the individual depravity of man. From the New Testament, he has amassed a formidable array of passages whose grammatical sense does not preclude their being taken individualistically, e.g. John 3:3 "Except a man be born again ...", and Romans 7:24 "O wretched man that I am ..."[10] The heyday of Old Testament sermons in New England was over. Such New Testament passages (just as numerous Old Testament Psalms) could be understood as speaking of the individual or the group. What is revealing is that the earliest New England Puritans understood them to address the whole community (as twentieth scholars have increasingly done) while later generations narrowed their meaning to individuals.

UNDERSTANDING IMAGERY OF THE NEW TESTAMENT

AND COVENANT WITH THE INDIVIDUAL

A generation later, New England had culturally rejoined England, church control of the colony had long

been broken, and Edward's religion had turned away from
the salvation of the community to salvation of individuals. The scene was ripe for revivals; and they were
not long in coming. In both Sinners in the Hands of an
Angry God and Christ the Great Example, Edwards' imagery
and identification was primarily with the New Testament;
and he was followed in that focus by Hopkins and Emmons.
And his chief antagonist, Charles Chauncy, also shared
that focus but opposed revivals.[11]

Why was there this short burst of meaningful use
of the Old Testament at the very start of New England
religious experience? And why was there this shift to
a position similar to the conservative position in England from which the Puritans had fled? The shift was
obvious to the Puritans back in England. In 1652, Sir
Richard Saltonstall, a friend of John Cotton and a former
resident of New England, wrote to Cotton criticizing him
for persecution of non-conformists and suggesting that
Cotton not "practice those courses in a wilderness which
you went so far to prevent." Cotton answered "Do you
think the Lord hath crowned the state with so many vic-
tories that they should suffer so many miscreants to
pluck the crown of sovereignty from Christ's head?"[12]

The European Reformation and English Puritanism
emphasized the direct participation of the individual
in the life of redemption and as a result disrupted
the inevitably imperfect larger social institutions,
the church and the state. But when the Puritans went
to New England, they left the dialectical interaction
between a basically anarchistic reform movement and a
social structure unified by large social institutions,
and instead discovered themselves constructing a society
rather than protesting against its defects. They found
themselves in the same position as the ecclesiastical
conservatives in England. By the time of Jonathan Edwards,
the church had lost control over and preoccupation with
the prospering state and began a basically anarchistic

concern for individual salvation.

UNDERSTANDING IMAGERY IN PREACHING AND ARTS

Understanding the shifts of dominant imagery in preaching may illumine not only why changes of order occurred in worship but also why changes of imagery occurred in the music and visual art of that period and later periods. Such understanding may aid studies of the folk arts as well as the fine arts. Preaching may have readied the culture for the artistic imagery or inspired it. Clearly the shift to New Testament imagery occurred in preaching before hymns gained general acceptance in Puritan or Baptist churches. Acceptance of hymns stressing New Testament imagery may be related not only to similar imagery by then dominant in the preaching but also to the fact that many such English and American hymnbooks justified hymns for worship on the basis of the hymn sung at the end of the Lord's Supper; and so, such collections contained a very large number of hymns suitable for communion.[13] To allow further analysis of how hymns, sermons, and worship order interrelated, studies of seventeenth, eighteenth, and nineteenth century American psalms and hymns should note when there were shifts from corporate to individual imagery and address.

In popular visual arts, one may see the imagery occur in a subsequent generation or continue then when the imagery had disappeared in the preaching. This time lag may occur both because the artist's religious formation occurred in childhood but his or her artistic productivity was in adulthood and because many of the popular arts caterred to popular taste of the buying adult whose own imagery was formed in childhood. Such a time lag is evident in engravings of the eighteenth century and especially in lithographs of the nineteenth century. A preliminary survey of such prints reveals not only the preponderance of New Testament imagery among

the religious subjects treated but also the persistence
of such imagery or any Biblical imagery long after it
had been abandoned in most popular preaching. But the
persistence of such imagery may also be attributed to
the popularity of such imagery instilled by the printed
versions of older sermons in which the imagery was dominant. For parallels with the imagery of New England
Puritan sermons, the lithographs of E.B. and E.C. Kellogg
are most germane; for that Hartford Connecticut firm,
second only to Currier and Ives in sales volume, caterred
to the New England taste in particular and dealt with
more religious themes than the New York based Currier
and Ives. From study of the full corpus of Kellogg
lithographs at the Connecticut Historical Society in
Hartford and at the Peters' collection in the Museum of
History and Technology, Washington D.C., it is clear
that Old Testament imagery is nearly absent from that
popular visual art form and New Testament imagery is
prolific.[14]

When studying nineteenth century American lithographs
with an eye to religious theme and iconographic detail,
one discovers that the largest configuration of lithographs (from the beginning of lithography in the 1830's
until the Civil War) features the devil in political
caricatures as Andrew Jackson was portrayed in "Office
Hunters for the Year 1834," an 1834 lithograph reproduced
on the cover of this book. But the largest confivation
of lithographs (from the 1870's and later) features irregularities in personal relations. These configurations
are all the more striking when one looks for English,
French, or German precedents and discovers far less use
of the devil in either the eighteenth or nineteenth century prints in those countries. In American prints, the
devil appears not only much more often but also much more
at center stage than in European prints; and most significantly, the devil in American prints is personified
as the major political leader such as the president. (In

European prints, the devil may occasionally stand close
to the leader but was not personified as the actual political leader.)[15]

The shift of focus in art from the political life
to the personal life corresponds to the shifts in preaching and worship order we have studied in this volume,
although there is a delayed reaction in the development
of both configurations for reasons discussed earlier
in this section. American sermons help us understand
why American artists would portray strong political
leaders as the devil while European artists would not.
A theme repeated in seventeenth and eighteenth century
American sermons was drawn from the thirteenth chapter
of the book of Revelation. John Cotton had noted "All
rulers are the beast ... If you tether a beast at night,
he knows the length of his tether before morning."[16]
The moral was to make short tethers and keep them tight
in relation to leaders of both the church and state. In
his Massachusetts' election sermon of 1776 (back in Boston
after the British evacuation), Samuel West demonstrated
that the theme was still a lively one over a hundred years
later:

> Most sacred certainly belongs only to God alone,
> -- yet how common it is to see this title or
> ones like it given to rulers! And how often
> have we been told that the ruler can do no wrong!
> Even though he should be so foolish and wicked
> as hardly capable of ever being in the right,
> yet still it must be asserted and maintained
> that it is impossible for him to do wrong! The
> cruel, savage disposition of tyrants, and the
> idolatrous reverence paid them, are both most
> beautifully exhibited to view by the apostle
> John in Revelation, thirteenth chapter ... The
> apostle gives description of a horrible wild
> beast ... To this beast we find the dragon
> gave his power ... this is to denote that ty-
> rants are the ministers of Satan.[17]

In the early seventeenth century, sermon images and
texts as well as worship orders stressed God's covenant
with the people who were responsible in shaping the church
worship and the wider community development. In the later

seventeenth century, the sermon images and texts and the
worship orders began to shift away from such responsibility. By the early nineteenth century, the sermon
imagery and texts and the worship orders had largely
eliminated such responsibility by focusing more narrowly
on converting the individual. Images in the arts reflected and informed some of these shifts; and lithographs such as "Office Hunters for the Year 1834" remind
the viewer of the wider concerns and responsibilities
called forth in early American free church worship.

BIBLE QUOTATIONS IN NEW ENGLAND SERMONS

Preacher	Cotton	Willard	Willard	I.Mather	Edwards	Edwards	Hopkins	Emmons	Chauncy	Mayhew
Sermon Title	God's Promise	Sermon Ezekiel	The Duty	Birth Sins	Sinners In Hands	Christ Good	Impor-tance	Ra-tional	Chris-tian	Dis-course
Evans Number	402	277	296	2053	4713	6492	10928		12717	
Date	1634	1679	1680	1719	1741	1749	1768		1773	1750
O.T.Narrative: People of God	T26	35	T5 (2)	9	2	0	0	0	0	0
O.T.Prophecy	19	T28	7	8	T9(1)	6	2	0	1	0
O.T.Wisdom	2	1	0	6	3	2	2	0	0	0
O.T.Psalms of Individual Lament	0	0	3	2	0	0	0	0	0	0
TOTAL O.T.	47	64	15	25	14	8	4	0	1	0
N.T.Quotation of or Allusion to O.T.	4(1)	3	0	3	4	0	0	0	0	0
N.T.Narrative: People of God	3(1)	0	1 (1)	1	0	0	0	T3	T5	0
N.T.Teaching (parables, exhortations)	3	0	3	2	1	1	0	0	3	1(1)
N.T.Individual as example	3	0	0	0	0	4	0	0	0	0
N.T.Abstract Theology(Paul, John, Hebrews)	0	0	2	17(1)	3(1)	5	T25	14	8(3)	0
N.T.Christ as Example,Nature of Leadership, Our Commission	0	0	0	0	0	T32	3	0	5	0
TOTAL N.T.	13	3	5	23	8	42	28	17	21	1
TOTAL BIBLE	60	67	20	48	22	50	32	17	22	1

BIBLE QUOTATIONS IN OLD ENGLAND SERMONS

Preacher	Hooker	Andrewes	Andrewes	Laud	Laud	Cartwright	Perkins	Ames	Cotton
Sermon Title	Remedy Against	Resurrection	On the Third	Birthday	Accession	Speech at Contract	Discourse	Substance	Way of Life
Number in Works	V3,N4	V3,N17	V5,N2	N1	N2	Cartwrightiana, 1951	T.Meril ed.1966	London, 1659	
Date	1590	1623	1592	1621	1621	1595	1596	<1633	<1630
O.T.Narrative: People of God	1	11	58	20	11	16	22	4	4
O.T.Prophecy	4	30	20	7	T9	0	19	5	3
O.T.Wisdom	4	2	7	1	3	1	17	2	4
O.T.Psalms of Individual Lament	2			2	1	0	5	T4	3
TOTAL O.T.	12	46	86	37	24	17	63	15	14
N.T.Quotation of or Allusion to O.T.	0	0	0	0	0	0	0	0	0
N.T.Narrative: People of God	1	3	4	3	1	1	10	1	3
N.T.Teaching (parables, exhortations)	T5	13	6	4	6	14	48	T13	16
N.T.Individual as example	0	0	0	0	0	0	5	0	0
N.T.Abstract Theology (Paul, John, Hebrews)	0	17	12	0	1	0	96	T4	5
N.T.Christ as Example, Nature of Leadership	2	5	0	0	0	0	0	0	1
TOTAL N.T.	8	42	22	9	8	15	159	18	25
TOTAL BIBLE	20	88	108	46	32	32	222	33	39

NOTES

The extensiveness of these notes makes unnecessary
a separate bibliographic essay, although a selected bibliography follows the notes.

PREFACE

1. The best of such books (e.g. Alice Baldwin's The
New England Clergy and the American Revolution, Durham
Duke University Press, 1928) make no pretense of knowing
worship order and conduct; and the worst of such books
(e.g. Ola Winslow's Meetinghouse Hill: 1630-1783, New
York, Macmillan Company, 1952) generalize what little
evidence they acquire and read later seventeenth, eighteenth, and even nineteenth century forms back into the
early seventeenth century so as to present a monolithic
Puritan form of worship without discernible development.
This latter procedure flaws also Charles Hambrick-Stowe's
work; for he mixes late seventeenth century practices by
John Norton and Cotton Mather with only selected parts
of much earlier seventeenth century practices by John
Cotton and so presents a false undifferentiated pattern
of Puritan worship for a wide period of time: cf. "Spiritual Dynamics of Puritan Worship," New England Meeting
House and Church: 1630-1850, edited by Peter Benes, Boston, Boston University, 1980, pp. 112-123. And by over
attention to the sermon, he judges the morning and afternoon worship as nearly identical; but in fact, the character of substantial lay participation made the two services significantly different: i.e. the lay questioning
and exhorting (that Hambrick-Stowe fails to mention) in
the morning worship could be as wide ranging as the sermon's scope; but the frequent lay relations of regeneration and confessions (that Hambrick-Stowe fails to mention) in the afternoon worship were narrower in scope.
This difference is important in distinguishing later developments noted in Chapter Four, page 99. There are mis-
leading statements by Hambrick-Stowe: e.g. Thomas Lechford's Plain Dealing, Or Newes from New England is hardly
"dispassionate" (p.116); the sacrament of the Lord's
Supper was not "monthly or bi-monthly" (p.116) as the
bi-monthly celebration was abnormal and the monthly one
much more common; and admission of new members occurred
frequently and not "occasionally" (p.116) in afternoon
worship. Philip Zimmerman's article that accompanies Hambrick-Stowe's (cf. "The Lord's Supper in Early New England: The Setting and Service," pp. 124-134) is based
on wider research, recognizes pluralism in worship forms,
and shares some insights on development in communion form

and does not try to present the practices as monolithic;
but greater attention to church record books and histories
would help him avoid some errors: e.g. on pages 130-131,
he mistakenly asserts that Samuel Sewell was instrumental
in persuading James Allen ... to return /First Church Bos-
ton7 to a monthly schedule in 1705" for the celebration of
communion. At the time of the 1705 conversation, First
Church was already celebrating the Lord's Supper on the
first Sunday of each month, a pattern Davenport had instituted to replace the much earlier pattern of celebrating communion every four Sundays. Sewell preferred the
latter pattern not only because it honored each Lord's Day
(as Zimmerman notes) but also because it allowed him to
take communion more often than once a month. But First
Church did not change their pattern after Sewell's discussion with Allen. For further discussion of this matter,
see Chapter Four, pages 82-84.
    2. Besides Perry Miller's well known volumes on
Puritan theology, there are more specialized works such
as E. Brooks Holifield's fine The Covenant Sealed: The
Development of Puritan Sacramental Theology in old and
New England, 1570-1720, New Haven, Yale University Press,
1974. Three volumes mention some early worship practices
within a primary attention to theological developments:
Robert Wall's Massachusetts Bay: The Crucial Decade, 1640-
1650, New Haven, Yale University Press, 1972; David Hall's
The Faithful Shepherd: A History of the New England Ministry In The Seventeenth Century, Chapel Hill, University of
North Carolina Press, 1972; and David Lewis Beebe, The
Seals of the Covenant: The Doctrine and Place of the Sacraments and Censures in the New England Puritan Theology
Underlying the Cambridge Platform of 1648, Th.D. disserta-
tion, Pacific School of Religion, 1966. The volume giving
most attention to worship practices is C. C. Goen's Reviv-
alism and Separatism In New England, 1740-1800: Strict
Congregationalists and Separate Baptists In The Great
Awakening, New Haven, Yale University Press, 1962; but
Goen's work does not deal with the origins of worship
practices in the first hundred years. Winton U. Solberg's
Redeem The Time: The Puritan Sabbath In Early America
(Cambridge, Harvard University Press, 1977) is a study of
the philosophies and policies of Sabbatarianism; but while
that volume describes at length what one was not to do on
the Sabbath, it does not describe what one was to do in
worship.
    3. Julius Melton's Presbyterian Worship in America:
Changing Patterns Since 1787 (Richmond, John Knox Press,
1967) is helpful in discussing directories of worship recommended to Presbyterian churches even before the revised
directory for worship was adopted by the 1788 General Assembly; but he admits little knowledge of how Presbyterians actually worshipped before or even after that late
eighteenth century directory was adopted. Gerald De
Jong's The Dutch Reformed Church In The American Colonies

(Grand Rapids, Wm. B. Eerdmans, 1978) gives the worship
pattern used in many churches in Holland and asserts
that new world churches conformed to it. But he provides
little evidence from church records to document local
church practices. Numerous references in the six volume
Ecclesiastical Records, State of New York (Albany, James
B. Lyon, 1901-1905) witness to use of the liturgy from
Holland when there was a minister available. But there
were also ample instances where a shortage of ministers
left laity to lead modified worship in the area that
became New York colony; and beginning in 1683, Guiliam
Bertholf was the only Dutch Reformed minister in New
Jersey and was using laity in worship leadership ways
not acceptable in much of New York.
    4. Cf. Doug Adams, "Free Church Worship in America
From 1620 to 1835," Worship (September, 1981) Volume 55,
Number 5, pp. 436-440; and Doug Adams, "Changing Biblical
Imagery and American Identity In Seventeenth and Eigh-
teenth Century Sermons and Arts," Papers for the Annual
Meeting of the American Academy of Homiletics, ed. Charles
Rice, Atlanta, American Academy of Homiletics, 1982.

                        INTRODUCTION

    1. The Separatist patterns are detailed in The Works
of John Robinson, Robert Ashton, ed., Boston, Doctrinal
Tract and Book Society, 1851, 3 volumes; and the Puritan
patterns are detailed in John Cotton's works, especially
The True Constitution of a Particular Visible Church
Proved By Scripture, London, 1642 and The Way of the
Churches of Christ in New England, London, 1645. Works
such as Winthrop's Journals, James Hosmer, ed. (New York,
Barnes and Noble, 1953) provide important connections
between Separatist and Puritan worship. Records of each
local church sometimes provide details of worship order
when changes were voted.
    2. James F. White, Protestant Worship and Church
Architecture, New York, Oxford University Press, 1964,
p. 124.
    3. Doug Adams, "Religion in Revolution: Bicentennial
Perspectives on Increasing Personal Participation in Worship and the World: 1776 and 1976," Liturgy, Vol. 20,
No. 3 (March, 1975) pp. 72-75; and "The Question Period
and Authority in Seventeenth and Eighteenth Century
American Religion," Abstracts of AAR and SBL Pacific
Northwest Region Annual Meeting: May 6-8, 1976, University of Oregon, Eugene, 1976, p. 18.
    4. For the theology and practice among the Disciples,
consult Alexander Campbell, The Christian System In
Reference To the Union of Christians and Restoration of
Primitive Christianity As Plead By the Current Reformation, St. Louis, Christian Publishing Company, 1839,
especially pp. 351 ff.

CHAPTER I

1. Marginal scriptural citations were a paper saving
device; and it was understood that they should be read
in full at the indicated places as they had been, for
instance, if the manuscript was based on a public lecture
or sermon.

2. John Cotton, The True Constitution of a Particular Visible Church Proved by Scripture, London, 1642,
pp. 5-8. This work was probably written in 1634-1635
according to Larzer Ziff, The Career of John Cotton:
Puritanism and The American Experience, Princeton, Princc-
ton University Press, 1962, p. 266.

3. John Cotton, The Way of the Churches of Christ
in New England, London, 1645, p. 66. Ziff notes that
Cotton wrote this work a few years earlier without in-
tending its publication, which was provoked because of
Presbyterian attacks on circulating manuscripts of it.
Ziff, op.cit., p. 191.

4. Thomas Lechford, Plain Dealing or News from New
England, London, Johnson Reprint Corporation, 1969, p. 45.
The work was originally published in London in 1642. New
England Puritans had a low regard for Lechford and his
work.

5. Cotton, The Way of the Churches of Christ in New
England, op.cit., pp. 66-67.

6. If the prayers were later in the service, as in
the Dutch Reformed churches, the papers were passed to
a deacon who conveyed them to the minister for incor-
poration into the prayer after the sermon. (cf. Gerald
DeJong, The Dutch Reformed Church in the American Colonies, Grand Rapids, Wm. B. Eerdmans, 1978, p. 132.) No
such bills or notes from First Church survive from that
early period; but specimens of later prayer notes were
preserved by Cotton Mather at Old North Church; e.g.
"Benjamin Elton bound to sea desires prayers for him,
that God would bless and prosper him and in safety re-
turne him." "Anne Williams would return thanks to God
for hire safe deliverance in child bead, and desires
your prayers for hir absent husband abroad at see."
Although Mather included such notes in his public prayers,
he also presented "the particular cases, there exhibited,
before the Lord, in my study, where I may more particularly implore the grace of God, for each of them, than
I did in the public." Diary of Cotton Mather, New York,
Frederick Ungar Publishing Company, I,pp. 62-63. Samuel
Sewall provides the text of a number of his and others'
prayer notes which usually concerned the health of family
members. M. Halsey Thomas, The Diary of Samuel Sewall,
New York, Farrar, Straus and Giroux, 1973, I, p. 141 and
II, pp. 697, 699, 763-764, 816, 864, 951, 1020. Some
notes would be sent to more than one church; e.g. I,
p. 141 and II, pp. 951, 1002, and 1020. He sent up notes
in numerous other worship services; e.g. I, pp. 264 and
324 and II, pp. 720, 787, 793, 824, 825, 941. And he
mentions the prayer notes sent up by others; e.g. I,

pp. 98 and 327 and II, pp. 659, 695, 742, 858, and 1016.
On one occasion, he arrived too late to give his prayer
to the minister (II, p. 787); but in only one instance,
did he record that the minister failed to include his
note: "I put up a note to pray for the Indians that
light might be communicated to them by the candlestick,
but my note was with the latest, and so not professedly
prayed for at all." (I, p. 59).

7. John Cotton, The Way of the Churches of Christ in
New England, op.cit., p. 67.

8. J. Spencer Curwen, Studies in Worship Music, London, 1888, p. 111.

9. Percy A. Scholes, The Puritans and Music in England and New England, London, Oxford University Press,
1934, p. 259.

10. The most common tunes were known as Oxford, York,
Litchfield, Windsor, St. David's, and Martyrs. Curwen,
op.cit., p. 111.

11. Cotton, Singing of Psalms, a Gospel Ordinance
(London, 1650) p. 62. Earlier in England, Cotton had
opposed such reading of psalms. A Practical Commentary
or an Exposition ... Upon the First Epistle Generall
of John, London, 1656, p. 157.

12. Cotton, Singing of Psalms, op.cit., pp. 40 and 43.
Cotton would allow in worship as lawful all spiritual
songs in Scripture (Songs of Moses, Solomon, Elizabeth,
and Mary, et.al. as well as David) p. 15. But he saw
the hymn at the Last Supper as a Hebrew psalm, p. 8.

13. Richard D. Pierce, ed., The Records of the First
Church in Boston 1630-1868, Publication of the Colonial
Society of Massachusetts, Boston, 1961, Vol. 39, p. 52.

14. Ibid., p. 56.

15. Cotton, Singing of Psalms, p. 40.

16. Ibid., p. 38; Letter, John Cotton to R. Levitt,
(in response to Levitt's inquiry of March 3, 1625) Massachusetts Historical Collections, 2nd Series, Volume X,
p. 183; and Pierce, ed.,The Records, op.cit., Vol. 39,
p. xlv.

17. Pierce, ed., op.cit.pp. 218, 222, and 223.

18. Thomas Walter, The Ground and Rules of Music
Explained or an Introduction to the Art of Singing by
Note, Fitted to the Meanest Capacity, Boston, 1721, p. 5.
Samuel Sewall bears witness to the less than harmonious
manner of Puritan singing; e.g. The Diary of Samuel
Sewall, op.cit., e.g. I, p. 538 and II, pp. 720, 881,
and 886. By the late seventeenth century, only a few
stanzas of a psalm might be sung; e.g. I, pp. 177 and
283 and II, pp. 661, 680, 816, 893, and 1064.

19. John Cotton, The Way of the Churches of Christ
in New England, op.cit., p. 67.

20. James Hosmer, ed., Winthrop's Journal, New York,
Barnes and Noble, 1953, Vol. I, p. 231.

21. Cotton Mather, Magnalia Christi Americana, Hartford, 1855, Book III, Chapter XVIII. Cf. Mather, Ratio
Disciplinae Fratrum Nov-Anglorum: A Faithful Account

of the Discipline Professed and Practised in the Churches
of New-England, Boston, 1726, p. 61.

22. John Cotton, Christ the Fountaine of Life, London, 1651, p. 181.

23. John Cotton, A Modest and Cleare Answer to Mr.
Ball's Discourse of Set Formes of Prayer, London, 1642,
p. 28.

24. Hosmer, ed., Winthrop's Journal, op.cit., II,
pp. 69-70.

25. Ibid., I, p. 60.

26. Ibid., p. 145.

27. Ibid., p. 123.

28. John Cotton, The True Constitution, op.cit.,
p. 6.

29. Hosmer, Winthrop's Journal, op.cit., II, pp.
144-145.

30. Charles Francis Adams, Three Episodes of Massachusetts History, Boston, Houghton Mifflin Company, 1894,
p. 401.

31. Robert Ashton, ed., The Works of John Robinson,
Boston, Doctrinal Tract and Book Society, 1851, III,
p. 327.

32. Hosmer, Winthrop's Journal, op.cit., I, p. 232.

33. Ibid., p. 234.

34. Ibid., p. 209.

35. David Hall, ed, The Antinomian Controversy,
1636-1638: A Documentary History, Middletown, Wesleyan
University Press, 1968, p. 209.

36. Ibid., II, p. 324. Preaching the word was called
an ordinance, although we think of the term more commonly
applied to the sacraments of baptism and Lord's Supper.
John Cotton, The Way of the Churches of Christ in New-England, op.cit., p. 66.

37. Hosmer, Winthrop's Journal, op.cit., II, p. 324.
Winthrop noted that "divers were offended at his zeal in
some of these passages."

38. Nathaniel Shurtleff, ed., Records of the Governor and Company of the Massachusetts Bay in New England,
Boston, 1853, 4, pt. 1, pp. 122, 151, 156-157, 194, 215,
and 313.

39. Cotton, Way of the Churches of Christ in New-England, op.cit., p. 68.

40. Ibid., p. 69.

41. Ibid., pp. 69-70.

42. Ibid., pp. 68-69.

43. Lechford, Plain Dealing, op.cit., p. 46.

44. John Cotton, The Way of Congregational Churches
Cleared, London, 1648, p. 67. For Cotton's low opinion
of Lechford and his Plain Dealing see pp. 71-72.

45. Ziff, op.cit., p. 199 and 189. Cf. John Davenport, An Answer of the Elders of the Severall Churches
in New-England unto Nine Positions Sent Over to Them,
London, 1643; and Richard Mather, Church-government and
Church-covenant Discussed, London, 1643.

46. Lechford, op.cit., p. 46.

47. Ibid., p. 44.

48. We do not know the exact number of regular worshippers or even the number of regular communicants in
Cotton's meetinghouse, except that there were growing
numbers that required the building of a larger meetinghouse in 1640. Nothing is known of the meetinghouse's
dimensions. (cf. Marian Card Donnelly, The New England
Meeting Houses of the Seventeenth Century, Middletown,
Wesleyan Univeristy Press, 1968, p. 13.) The difficulty
in determining exact numbers of communicants arises from
the state of church records in the years 1630-1633; for
the notations about termination of members were added
in 1650 without specifying when the deaths or dismissals
to other locations occurred, with the exception of dismissals to the Charlestown Church. Pierce, ed., Records,
op.cit., Vol. 39, pp. 13-16. When Cotton was ordained
as teacher of the Boston church in 1633, there were between 105 and 125 church members; but in the course of
his ministry, 1034 children were baptized and 652 adults
were admitted into membership. As members needed com-
pelling reasons for not being in worship and as members'
children and nonmembers probably at least doubled the
size of the worshipping community, Cotton worshipped
with a substantial number of persons; but severe weather
could minimize the numbers in winter months.

CHAPTER II

1. Lechford, op.cit., pp. 47-51.
2. Cotton, The Way of the Churches of Christ in New-
England, op.cit., p. 69. But in a sermon of May 2, 1639,
Cotton opposed civil government support of minister's
salaries as Winthrop carefully noted. Winthrop, Winthrop's Journal, op.cit., I, p. 299.
3. Marian Card Donnelly, The New England Meeting
House of the Seventeenth Century, op.cit., pp. 16 add 46.
4. Cotton, The Way of the Churches of Christ in New-
England, op.cit., p. 69.
5. For an example of the attached table during that
period, cf. Donnelly, op.cit., p. 138.
6. Pierce, ed., Records, op.cit., Vol 39, pp. liv-lv.
7. Horton Davies, Worship and Theology in England
From Andrewes to Baxter and Fox, 1603-1690, Princeton,
Princeton University Press, 1975, pp. 10-11.
8. Donnelly, op.cit., p. 69 gives one example of
such expansion.
9. Cotton, The Way of the Churches of Christ in New-
England, op.cit., p. 68.
10. Winthrop, Winthrop's Journal, op.cit., I, p. 107.
11. Pierce, ed., Records, op.cit., Vol. 39, pp. 278-
324.
12. Pierce, ed., Records, op.cit., Vol. 39, p. 290.
13. Cotton, The Way of the Churches of Christ in New-
England, op.cit., p. 69.

14. Pierce, ed., Records, op.cit., pp. 208 and 210.
Alice Morse Earle's intriguing accounts of offerings need
to be carefully verified: besides libelous verses and
Quaker messages, she enumerates broken worthless wampum
that occasioned a 1651 New Haven vote to accept only silver and bills in the box. She describes John Rogers de-
riding a pompous New London minister by throwing an old
periwig into the box, and "one Puritan goodwife, sternly
unforgiving, never saw a contribution taken for prosely-
ting the Indians without depositing in the contribution-
box a number of leaden bullets, the only tokens she
wished to see ever dispersed among the Redmen." The
Sabbath in Puritan New England, New York, Charles Scribner's Sons, 1896, pp. 117-118.
15. Chapter VII, sections 3 and 4 of "Platform of
Church Discipline" in Congregational Order: The Ancient
Platforms of the Congregational Churches of New England,
Hartford, Edwin Hunt, 1845, p. 112.
16. Esdras Read served the Wenham church (that
merged with Clemsford) from 1644 to 1653 when he was
removed under a cloud. Robert G. Pope, ed., The Notebook of the Reverend John Fiske, 1644-1675 (Publications
of the Colonial Society of Massachusetts) Boston, 1974,
XLVII, pp. 95-96. See also pages 47 and 56 for charges
against him in 1646 and 1648. Two of Boston's First
Church deacons were dismissed from office in 1668 over
irregularities in the calling of John Davenport to be
pastor. Pierce, ed., op.cit., p. 62.
17. Pierce, op.cit., pp. 16-55. While correct on
the number of church admissions, William Emerson made
faulty calculations of excommunications and so led Larzer
Ziff astray into underestimating the frequency and significance of that exercise. Cf. Ziff, op.cit., p. 252
and William Emerson, An Historical Sketch of the First
Church of Boston, Boston, 1812, pp. 81-82.
18. Chapter XII, sections 2-5, Congregational Order,
op.cit., pp. 127-128.
19. Hosmer, Winthrop's Journal, op.cit., I, p. 107.
20. Pope, The Notebook, op.cit., p. 4.
21. Ibid., pp. 36-37.
22. Ibid., pp. 6-7.
23. Nathaniel Morton, New-Englands Memorial: Or,
A Brief Relation of the Most Memorable and Remarkable
Passages of the Providence of God, Manifested to the
Planters of New-England in America; With Special Reference to the First Colony Thereof, Called New-Plimouth,
Cambridge, 1669, p. 10. See also Cotton Mather, Magnalia
Christi Americana, Cambridge, The Belknap Press of Harvard
University Press, 1977, Book I, Ch. IV, pp. 146-147.
24. Lechford, Plain Dealing, op.cit., p. 23. At
Wenham (Chelmsford), the practice of women speaking their
own relations in Sunday worship was continued until the
end of the 1650s; and by the 1660s even some of the men
were allowed to write out their relations for the pastor
to read in worship. Pope, The Notebook, op.cit., p. xvii
and passim.

25. Richard D. Pierce, ed., The Records of the First
Church in Salem Massachusetts 1629-1736, Salem, Essex
Institute, 1974, p. xvii.

26. John Cotton, A Treatise of the Covenant of Grace,
London, 1659, pp. 199-200.

27. Pierce, ed., The Records of the First Church in
Boston, op.cit., Vol. 39, p. 12.

28. Pierce, ed., The Records of the First Church in
Salem Massachusetts 1629-1736, op.cit., pp. 3-5.

29. Some Westminster sections on church discipline
were rejected and amended by the Cambridge Platform: i.e.
chapters 25, 30, and 31. Congregational Order, op.cit.,
pp. 76-77.

30. Pope, The Notebook, op.cit., p. 11.

31. Pierce, ed., The Records of the First Church in
Salem, op.cit., pp. 89 and 151.

32. John Cotton, The Way of the Churches of Christ
in New-England, op.cit., p. 58.

33. Cf. Cotton Mather, Magnalia, London, 1702, Book
IV, Ch. 4, p. 159, Lechford, op.cit., p. 22.

34. Pastor Higginson's son John was examined and
voted into membership of the Salem church at age 14.
Pierce, ed., The Records of the First Church in Salem,
op.cit., p. xivn. At the Wenham church, "the children
of church members under the age of 14 or 15 years when
their parents took the covenant are included in their
parents' covenant" and could be baptized. Pope, op.cit.,
p. 110. But one should not infer that persons over fifteen years of age would not be eligible for baptism except by qualifying for membership. If either of their
parents were members, even those of age could be bap-
tised at Salem. Pierce, ed., The Records of the First
Church in Salem, op.cit., pp. 112-113. There are rare
instances of adult baptism as those without any previous
church connection became full members in the late seventeenth century; but such instances were much more common
in the eighteenth century. Pierce, ed., The Records of
the First Church in Boston, op.cit., Vol. 39, pp. 77,
94, 98, 101-115.

35. Ibid., I, p. 40. Cf. Cambridge Platform, Chapter
XIII, Section 7, Congregational Order, op.cit., p. 133.

36. Pope, op.cit., p. 21.

37. Ibid., pp. 18-19.

38. Congregational Order, op.cit., p. 131.

39. Ibid., pp. 131-132.

40. Ibid., pp. 131-132.

41. Ibid., p. 137.

42. Pierce, Records of the First Church in Boston,
op.cit., pp. 21-22, 25, 34, 49, 52-54.

43. Ibid., pp. 22, 32, 42, 46, and 48.

44. Ibid., pp. 20, 28, 31, 37-39, 41, 42, 44-46,
and 49.

45. Ibid., pp. 22, 28-30, 34, 64, and 66.

46. Ibid., pp. 52-55, 59, and 61.

47. Ibid., pp. 44, 59, 66, 71, and 77-78.

48. Ibid., pp. 44-47, and 53.

49. Ibid., p. 42.
50. Ibid., pp. 44 and 57.
51. Ibid., pp. 26-27.
52. Ibid., pp. 36, 52, and 53.
53. Ibid., p. 46. William Francklyn was excommunicated in the latter way. But many of the entries on
church consent to excommunications do not specify whether
the consent was by silence or show of hands; so, we do
not conclusively know the extent of either method.
54. Hosmer, Winthrop's Journal, op.cit., I, p. 248.
Pages 242-255 give a lengthy description of the whole
proceeding held on a lecture day.
55. Ibid., pp. 25-30, 44, and 47. Only one of the
foregoing persons was later a subject of church discussion: John Webb was excommunicated in 1655 for withdrawing from his wife and attempting uncleanness. Ibid.,
p. 61.
56. Ibid., p. 29.
57. John Cotton, The Way of the Churches of Christ
in New-England, op.cit., p. 70.

CHAPTER III

1. Hosmer, Winthrop's Journal, op.cit., I, pp. 93-94.
2. Henry Ainsworth's Defence of the Holy Scriptures,
Worship and Ministrie Used in the Christian Churches Se-
parated from Antichrist: Against the Challenges, Cavils,
and Contradiction of Mr. Smythe as quoted in part in B.
Hanbury, Historical Memorials Relating to the Independents,
London, 1839, Vol. I, p. 181.
3. Letter of the Bromheedes to Sir William Hammerton,
Harleian Ms. 360 fol. 71 recto in the British Museum. In
quoting this passage, Horton Davies noted the similarity
of this pattern of prophesying to the weekday instruction
of pastors in Zwingli's Zurich and Puritan pastors in
Elizabethan England; but in Amsterdam, the pattern was
instituted for regular Sunday worship and enlarged to
include the congregation. Horton Davies, Worship and
Theology In England From Andrewes to Baxter and Fox,
1603-1690, op.cit., pp. 500-501.
4. Ashton, ed., op.cit., III, p. 485.
5. Ibid., II, p. 142. The passage appeared in
Robinson's A Justification of Separation from the Church
of England Against Mr. Richard Bernard His Invective,
Intitled The Separatist's Schisme.
6. He marshals the arguments and biblical passages
most concisely in his 1625 publication A Just and Necessary Apology of Certain Christians, No Less Contumeliously
than Commonly Called Brownists or Barrowists, Chapter VIII
"Of the Exercise of Prophecy," reprinted in Ashton, op.
cit., III, pp. 55-58. See also Ashton, II, pp. 246-251;
and III, pp. 324-331 and 431-433.
7. Ibid., III, p. 55.
8. Ibid., III, p. 58.

9. Ibid., III, p. 134.
10. For these and other similarities between early Baptists and Quakers, cf. William Tallack, George Fox, the Friends, and the Early Baptists, London, 1868; and Davies, op.cit., pp. 490-521.
11. Ibid., III, p. 329; cf. p. 326.
12. When Smythe and his followers baptized each other in Amsterdam, they did not have prayers until after the sacrament was administered. Ashton, op.cit., III, pp. 168-169. The mode of baptism was not at issue then, for immersion was not known until 1620 in Holland. Davies, op.cit., p. 499.
13. Ibid., pp. 180-181.
14. John Smith, Paralleles, Censures, Observations (n.p., 1609) p. 56.
15. William Bradford, Bradford's History of Plimouth Plantation, Boston, Wright and Potter, 1901, p. 194.
16. Ibid., p. 200.
17. Ashton, op.cit., III, pp. 22-25. Cf. II, p. 246 for Robinson's warrants for allowing an unordained person to pray as well as preach in public worship.
18. Bradford, op.cit., p. 493.
19. Ashton, op.cit., III, p. 488.
20. DeJong, The Dutch Reformed Church in the American Colonies, op.cit., p. 132; William Maxwell, A History of Worship in the Church of Scotland, London, Oxford University Press, 1955, p. 125; and Davies, op.cit., p. 457.
21. Ashton, op.cit., II, pp. 245 and 133.
22. Ibid., p. 241.
23. Ibid., p. 254.
24. Ibid., III, pp. 39ff.
25. Bradford, op.cit., p. 316.
26. e.g. Perry Miller, Orthodoxy in Massachusetts, 1630-1650, A Genetic Study, Cambridge, Harvard University Press, 1933, pp. 127-137; and Robert M. Bartlett, The Faith of the Pilgrims: An American Heritage, New York, United Church Press, 1978, pp. 305-321.
27. John Cotton, The Way of the Congregational Churches Cleared, op.cit., p. 195.
28. Bradford, op.cit., p. 332; and Ashton, op.cit., I, xlv.
29. Edward Winslow, Hypocrisie Unmasked, London, 1646, p. 92.
30. William Rathband, A Brief Narration of Some Courses (1694), pp. 54-55. Cf. Cotton Mather, Magnalia Christi Americana, Cambridge, Harvard University Press, 1977, Book I, Ch. IV, p. 153 on the Salem consultation with Plymouth to draw up the Salem church covenant and confession of faith.
31. Edmund Morgan, Roger Williams, The Church and the State, New York, Harcourt, Brace and World, 1967, pp. 29-33.
32. The Complete Writings of Roger Williams, New York, Russell and Russell, 1963, II, p. 272.
33. Ibid., III, p. 138.
34. Ibid., p. 225.

35. Morgan, op.cit., pp. 42-45; and The Complete Writings, op.cit., VII, pp. 130-131.
36. Roger Williams, The Hireling Ministry None of Christs, Or a Discourse Touching the Propagating the Gospel of Christ Jesus, London, 1652, reprinted in The Complete Writings, op.cit., VII, pp. 147-191; Henry Melville King, The Mother Church: A Brief Account of the Church and Early History of the First Baptist Church in Providence, Philadelphia, American Baptist Publication Society, 1897, p. 64.
37. The Complete Writings, op.cit., V, pp. 134-135; King, op.cit., p. 64.
38. The Complete Writings, op.cit., VII, p. 162; King, op.cit., pp. 22 and 45.
39. J. R. Graves, ed., The First Baptist Church, Memphis, Southern Baptist Book Store, 1890, p. 188; and Nathan Wood, The History of the First Baptist Church of Boston, Philadelphia, American Baptist Publication Society, 1899, p. 220.
40. Graves, op.cit., pp. 102 and 90-91; and Boyd, op.cit., pp. 34-35.
41. John Clarke, Ill Newes From New England: A Narration ..., London, 1652, pp. 9-10.
42. "Dunster MSS," p. 289, recorded in Wood, op.cit., p. 26.
43. Wood, op.cit., pp. 32-33, 29-42.
44. Ibid., p. 64.
45. Ibid., pp. 65-66.
46. Ibid., pp. 67 and 80.
47. Ibid., p. 136.
48. Ibid., p. 90.
49. Ibid., pp. 91, 39-51, 67-68, and 75-115.
50. Henry Burrage, "The Baptist Church in Kittery," Collections of Proceedings of the Maine History Society, Portland, Maine History Society, 1898, second series, IX, pp. 388-389. Cf. Wood, op.cit., pp. 179-183 for the precedence of this covenant. Dr. Robert Moody, ed., Province and Court Records of Maine, Portland, Maine History Society, 1947, III, p. 165 for court action attempting to stop the worship in Screven's Kittery home.
51. Hugh Barbour, The Quakers in Puritan England, New Haven, 1964, p. 8. Horton Davies noted that a number of English Quaker worship patterns may be traced back through the Baptists to the Mennonites of Holland; and the latter were the first Protestants using silent prayer in worship. Worship and Theology in England from Andrewes to Baxter and Fox, 1603-1690, Princeton, Princeton University Press, 1975, p. 497.
52. Robert Barclay, The Inner Life of the Religious Societies of the Commonwealth, London, 1879, third edition, p. 401.
53. Howard Brinton, Friends for 300 Years, New York, Harper and Row, 1952, p. 8.
54. M. Halsey Thomas, ed., The Diary of Samuel Sewall, New York, Farrar, Straus, and Giroux, 1973, I, p. 44. Cf.

pp. 67-68.

55. J. L. Nickalls, ed., The Journal of George Fox, Cambridge, 1952, I, p. 153.

56. Roger Williams, George Fox Digg'd Out of his Burrowes, The Complete Writing of Roger Williams, New York, Russell and Russell, 1963, VII, pp. 60-61.

57. John Burnyeat, "Journal of Life and Gospel Labours of John Burnyeat," 1691, in A Selected Series, Biographical Narrative, ed., John Barclay, London, 1839, Vol. 5, p. 50; Kenneth Carroll, John Perrot, Early Quaker Schismatic, London, 1971, pp. 69, 72, and 103-104; and George Selleck, Quakers in Boston, 1656-1964, Cambridge, Friends Meeting at Cambridge, pp. 26-28.

58. For example, Selleck, op.cit., p. 24 notes the lack of written records on the Boston Quaker worship.

59. Albert Cook Myers, Narratives of Early Pennsylvania, West New Jersey, and Delaware, 1630-1707, New York, Barnes and Noble, 1912, p. 271. George Keith may have been responsible for that time of the meeting, as he continued such a practice on his return to England. Ibid., pp. 335-337.

60. The Complete Writings of Roger Williams, op. cit., V, pp. 134-135.

61. Ibid., pp. 420 and 2-3. Cf. page xii for details of the Yearly Meeting.

62. Ibid., p. 162.

63. Ibid., p. 135.

64. Ibid., p. 140.

65. Ibid., pp. 361-363, 24, 134, and 210. Cf. Brinton, op.cit., pp. 89-90.

CHAPTER IV

1. Timothy Dwight, Theology Explained and Defended in a Series of Sermons, New York, Harper and Brothers, 1848, p. 356. Dwight shaped these sermons through two repetitions of the cycle as a pastor at Greenfield and two more of the cycle at Yale.

2. Charles Chauncy, Breaking of Bread in Remembrance of the Dying Love of Christ, a Gospel Institution. Five Sermons on the Lord's Supper, Boston, 1772.

3. Hosmer, ed., Winthrop's Journal, op.cit., I, p. 332.

4. Thomas, ed., The Diary of Samuel Sewall, op.cit., Vol. I, p. 521.

5. Ibid., I, p. 94 and II, pp. 810 and 1039.

6. Ibid., I, pp. 304, 419, 493 and II, pp. 698-699, 811, 839, 841, 849.

7. Donnelly, op.cit., p. 16. She was quoting from the Salem Town Records, p. 81. Town records frequently provide details of church architecture when additions were proposed or meeting houses were built.

8. Pierce, ed., The Records of the First Church in Salem, Massachusetts, 1629-1736, op.cit., pp. 87 and 142.

9. "Plymouth Church Records," Vol. I, Part II and Part V, Publications of the Colonial Society of Massachusetts, Boston, The Colonial Society of Massachusetts, 1920, XXII, pp. 145-178 and 255-263.
10. "Plymouth Church Records," Vol. I, Part III, op.cit., pp. 198-220.
11. "Plymouth Church Records," Vol. III, Publications of the Colonial Society of Massachusetts, Boston, The Colonial Society of Massachusetts, 1923, XXIII, pp. 558-559. Even when a church such as Chelmsford did not celebrate communion in winter months, it might acknowledge monthly communion (i.e. twelve celebrations per year) as the norm. Pope, ed., The Notebook, op.cit., p. 128.
12. Thomas, ed., The Diary of Samuel Sewall, op.cit., Vol. I, pp. 152-153. Cf. pp. 96, 161, 521 and II, pp. 650, 776, 779, 818, and perhaps 863. Also, he communed abroad as in I, pp. 214 and 241.
13. Ibid., I, p. 26.
14. Ibid., p. 36.
15. Ibid., p. 161. Cf. p. 40 and II, p. 905.
16. Cf. Michael G. Hall, ed., "The Autobiography of Increase Mather," Proceedings of the American Antiquarian Society, Worcester, 1962, Vol. 71, part 2, pp. 316-318; and Increase Mather, Practical Truths Tending to Promote the Power of Godliness, Boston, 1682, pp. 119ff.
17. Thomas, ed., The Diary of Samuel Sewall, op.cit., I, p. 528.
18. Ibid., p. 135.
19. Ibid., II, p. 779. Cf. p. 776.
20. Pope, ed., The Notebook, op.cit., pp. 109-110; and "Plymouth Church Records," op.cit., XXII, p. 172.
21. Pierce, ed., The Records of the First Church in Boston, op.cit., Vol. 39, pp. xxxi and 161; Vol. 40, p. 482.
22. Solomon Stoddard, An Appeal to the Learned ... Against the Exceptions of Mr. Mather, Boston, 1709, p. 2.
23. Increase Mather, A Call from Heaven to the Present and Succeeding Generations ..., Boston, 1679 and A Discourse Concerning the Danger of Apostasy ..., Boston, 1679.
24. Stoddard, An Appeal, op.cit., p. 53.
25. Soloman Stoddard, The Doctrine of Instituted Churches, Explained and Proved from the Word of God, London, 1700, p. 21.
26. Solomon Stoddard, The Safety of Appearing at the Day of Judgment in the Righteousness of Christ: Opened and Applied, Boston, 1687, pp. 338ff.
27. Stoddard, The Doctrine, op.cit., p. 22. Cf. Stoddard, An Appeal, op.cit., p. 63.
28. Increase Mather, A Dissertation, Wherein the Strange Doctrine Lately Published in a Sermon, the Tendency of which is to Encourage Unsanctified Persons (while such) to Approach the Holy Table of the LORD, is Examined and Confuted, Boston, 1708.
29. Especially see sermons VII and VIII in Norman S. Grabo, Edward Taylor's Treatise Concerning the Lord's

Supper, Michigan State University Press, 1966, pp. 171-221.

30. Solomon Stoddard, *The Doctrine*, op.cit., p. 19.
31. Stoddard, *An Appeal*, op.cit., pp. 52ff. Cf. Stoddard, *The Inexcusableness of Neglecting the Worship of God*, Boston, 1708.
32. Pierce, ed., *The Records of the First Church in Boston*, op.cit., Vol. 39, p. 213.
33. *Ibid.*, p. 159.
34. *Ibid.*, Vol. 40, p. 473.
35. *Ibid.*
36. *Ibid.*, p. 474.
37. *Ibid.*, p. 529.
38. *Ibid.*, pp. 531-532.
39. *Ibid.*, p. 551.
40. *Ibid.*, pp. 553-554.
41. "Plymouth Church Records," op.cit., XXII, p. 154.
42. *Ibid.*, p. 163.
43. *Ibid.*, pp. 337-338.
44. *Ibid.*, p. 386.
45. *Ibid.*, XXIII, pp. 574-575.
46. *Ibid.*, p. 580.
47. *Ibid.*, p. 591.
48. Pierce, ed., *The Records of the First Church in Salem, Massachusetts*, op.cit., p. 110.
49. *Ibid.*, p. 239.
50. *Ibid.*, p. 334.
51. Ralph Waldo Emerson, ed., *The Complete Works of Ralph Waldo Emerson*, Boston and New York, Houghton Mifflin Company, 1903-1904, XI, p. 24. Among other changed ways of thinking about communion, he proposed eliminating the actual physical elements and the statement that Jesus had instituted the Supper for all time.
52. Arthur Cushman McGiffert, Jr., ed., *Young Emerson Speaks: Unpublished Discourses on Many Subjects*, Boston, Houghton Mifflin Company, 1938, pp. 57-58.
53. Charles W. Baird, *The Presbyterian Liturgies, Historical Sketches*, Grand Rapids, 1960 Baker Book House, pp. 119 and 102.
54. *Ibid.*, p. 102.
55. *Ibid.*, p. 102.
56. Hosmer, op.cit., pp. 244-245; and cf. pp. 230-231.
57. Williston Walker, *The Creeds and Platforms of Congregationalism*, New York, 1893, p. 138. For more on Parker and Noyes' views, cf. Thomas Parker, *True Copy of a Letter Written by Mr. T. P. ... Declaring his Judgment Touching the Government Practised in the Churches of New England*, London, 1644; James Noyes, *The Temple Measured*, London, 1647; Lechford, op.cit., p. 56; and Robert Emmet Wall, Jr., *Massachusetts Bay: The Crucial Decade, 1640-1650*, New Haven, Yale University Press, 1972.
58. Thomas Hooker, *Survey of the Summe of Church Discipline*, London, 1648, pp. 36-37. Cf. Frank Shuffelton, *Thomas Hooker, 1586-1647*, Princeton, Princeton University Press, 1977.

59. Cotton Mather, <u>Magnalia Christi Americana</u>, New York, Russell and Russell, 1967, I, p. 349.
60. Thomas Hooker, <u>Survey</u>, <u>op.cit.</u>, Part II, pp. 16-18.
61. "The Trial of Ezekiel Cheever before the Church at New Haven ... 1649," <u>Collections</u>, Hartford, Connecticut Historical Society, 1860, I, pp. 29ff.
62. The Saybrook Platform is provided in full in <u>Congregational Order: The Ancient Platforms</u>, <u>op.cit.</u>, pp. 153-283. The minimizing interpretation by the New Haven Consociation is included as pp. 284-286. For discussion of the nearly unanimous rejection of the Saybrook Platform by the New London County churches, see S. Leroy Blake, <u>The Later History of the First Church of Christ</u>, New London, Connecticut, New London, 1900, p. 8.
63. Timothy Flint, <u>Recollections of the Last Ten Years</u>, Boston, Cummings, Hilliard, and Company, 1826, p. 117.
64. <u>Ibid.</u>, p. 117.
65. Charles Beecher, ed., <u>Autobiography, Correspondence, Etc., of Lyman Beecher, D.D.</u>, New York, Harper and Brothers, 1865, II, p. 572.
66. Reuben Tinker, <u>Sermons</u>, New York, A. Roman and Company, 1869, p. 251.
67. For a fuller discussion of this shift in attitude on reason, discussion, and questioning, see chapter four in Doug Adams' <u>Humor in the American Pulpit from George Whitefield Through Henry Ward Beecher</u>, Austin, The Sharing Company, 1981, pp. 147-196 and also pp. 92-98.
68. William Hubbard, <u>History of New England from the Year 1620 to the Year 1680</u>, Boston, Massachusetts Historical Society, 1848, pp. 65-66.
69. Williston Walker, <u>The Creeds and Platforms of Congregationalism</u>, Boston, Pilgrim Press, 1960, p. 405.
70. Thomas, ed., <u>The Diary of Samuel Sewall</u>, <u>op.cit.</u>, I, pp. 36-37.
71. For the "Manifesto" text, see Walker, <u>The Creeds</u>, <u>op.cit.</u>, pp. 472-480.
72. Cf. Increase Mather, <u>The Order of the Gospel, Professed and Practiced by the Churches of Christ in New England, Justified</u>, Boston, 1700.
73. Charles Grandison Finney, <u>Lectures on Revivals of Religion</u>, ed. by William G. McLoughlin, Cambridge, Belknap Press of Harvard University Press, 1960, p. 258. Finney may have been thinking of Solomon Stoddard who did approve lay preaching for those with "suitable abilities." Solomon Stoddard, <u>The Doctrine</u>, <u>op.cit.</u>, p. 16.
74. Jonathan Edwards, <u>Thoughts on the Revival of Religion in New England</u>, New York, American Tract Society, p. 325.
75. <u>Ibid.</u>, pp. 384ff.
76. Letter, Leonard Woods to William Sprague, (August 19, 1849), <u>Annals of the American Pulpit</u>, ed. by William B. Sprague, II, pp. 63-64.

77. Sprague, ed., Annals, op.cit., p. 302.
78. Letter, John Brigham to William Sprague, (September 15, 1855), Ibid., p. 263.
79. Letter, Chester Dewey to William Sprague, (April 26, 1852), Ibid., p. 21.
80. Letter, Leonard Withington to William Sprague, (February 1, 1856), Ibid., pp. 270-271.
81. Timothy Mather Cooley, Sketches of the Life and Character of the Rev. Lemuel Haynes, A.M., New York, Negro Universities Press, 1969, p. 117.
82. Jacob Knapp, Autobiography of Elder Jacob Knapp, New York, Sheldon and Company, 1868, p. 62.
83. Joshua Thomas, The American Baptist Heritage in Wales, Lafayette, Church History Research and Archives Affiliation, 1976, p. 58. For the question time among Baptists in the mid-seventeenth century in England, see The Life and Death of Mr. Henry Jessey, n.p., 1671, p. 40.
84. A. D. Gillette, ed., Minutes of the Philadelphia Baptist Association from 1707 to 1807, American Baptist Publication Society, 1851, p. 51. See also pp. 50 and 51.
85. Ibid., p. 27.
86. Cf. C. C. Goens, Revivalism and Separatism in New England, 1740-1800: Strict Congregationalists and Separate Baptists in the Great Awakening, New Haven and London, Yale University Press, 1962, pp. 296ff. and Errett Gates, The Early Relation and Separation of Baptists and Disciples, Chicago, The Christian Century Company, 1904, pp. 76ff.
87. Knapp, Autobiography, op.cit., p. 136.
88. H. K. Stimson, From the Stage Coach to the Pulpit, St. Louis, R. A. Campbell, 1874.
89. J. Mason Brewer, The Word on the Brazos: Negro Preacher Tales from the Brazos Bottoms of Texas, Austin, University of Texas Press, 1953, p. 62.
90. Henry Jackson, An Account of the Churches in Rhode Island, Providence, Whitney, 1854, p. 42.
91. Frances Wayland, Notes on the Principles and Practices of Baptist Churches, New York, Shelddon, Blakeman and Company, 1857, pp. 236-237.
92. A brief survey of eighteenth and nineteenth century Methodist policies is provided by John Bishop in "The Methodist Church: A Detailed Survey of its Worship," Methodist Worship in Relation to Free Church Worship, Scholars Studies Press, 1975, pp. 66-153. For worship in America, see especially pp. 71-75, 82-85 and 128-129. William Wade provides a comprehensive study of those policies and some key Methodist leaders: e.g. Francis Asbury and Joseph Pilmore. Wade's thesis shows that Asbury's lack of sacramental appreciation and preoccupation with episcopacy guided Methodism away from Wesley's original pattern that Pilmore more fully expressed. William Nash Wade, A History of Public Worship in the Methodist Episcopal Church and Methodist Episcopal Church, South, From 1789 to 1905, University of Notre Dame, Ph.D. dissertation, May, 1981. Cf. Frank Baker, From Wesley to Asbury: Studies in Early American

Methodism, Durham, Duke University Press, 1976. See
also Edwin E. Voigt, Methodist Worship in the Church
Universal, Nashville, Graded Press, 1965, pp. 70-83.
For the general outlines of Disciples' worship, see
Keith Watkins' brief but helpful "The Historic Disciple
Way," The Breaking of Bread: An Approach to Worship for
the Christian Churches, St. Louis, Bethany Press, 1966,
pp. 48-67; and Gates, The Early Relation and Separation
of Baptists and Disciples, op.cit., passim. While we
are well informed on Alexander Campbell's principles and
practices by those books and Campbell's own works (e.g.
The Christian System, op.cit., passim), there are many
unanswered questions about the origins of worship practiced by Barton Stone, the other main leader of groups
that formed the Disciples of Christ/Christian Church.
    93. John Wesley, A Consise Ecclesiastical History,
London, Paramore, 1781, IV, p. 174.
    94. George Whitefield, Fifteen Sermons Preached on
Various Important Subjects, Glascow, James Duncan and
Sons, 1792, p. 282.
    95. Joseph Gurney, ed., Eighteen Sermons Preached
by the Late Rev. George Whitefield, (taken verbatim in
short-hand and faithfully transcribed), Boston, 1820,
p. 238.
    96. Whitefield, Fifteen Sermons, op.cit., p. 156.
    97. Freeborn Garrettson, The Experience and Travels
of Mr. Freeborn Garrettson, Philadelphia, Hall, 1791,
pp. 171ff.; and cf. William Warren Sweet, Virginia Methodism, Richmond, Whittet and Shepperson, 1955, pp. 79ff.
    98. Francis Asbury, The Journal and Letters, ed.
Elmer T. Clark, J. Manning Potts, and Jacob S. Payton,
Nashville, Abingdon Press, 1958, II, p. 294.
    99. Joseph Pilmore, Journal, ed. Frederick E. Maser
and Howard T. Maag, Philadelphia, Message Publishing
Company, 1969, passim.
    100. Jesse Lee, A Short History of the Methodists in
the United States of America, Beginning in 1766, and
Continued Till 1809, Baltimore, Magill and Clime, 1810,
pp. 63-64.
    101. Ibid., p. 67.
    102. Ibid., pp. 67 and 90. But O'Kelly later left
the Methodist Episcopal Church to join the Republican
Methodist Church that manifested more concern for the
Lord's Supper frequent celebrations.
    103. John Wesley, Letters, ed. J. Telford, London,
Epworth Press, 1931, VII, p. 239.
    104. The Doctrines and Discipline of the Methodist
Episcopal Church, Philadelphia, Hall for Dickins, 1792,
pp. 24ff.
    105. Bishop, Methodist Worship, op.cit., p. 91.
    106. Proceedings of the Bishop and Presiding Elders
of the Methodist Episcopal Church in Council Assembled
at Baltimore, on the First Day of December, 1789, Baltimore, Goddard and Angell, 1789, pp. 6-7. Asbury only
noted taking communion five times between August 1771
and 1776. On June 1772, he observed "I was at the table

with Mr. Stringer. And many felt the power of God. But
I felt but little myself." And while he saw sacraments
as a duty, he announced, "they did not appear to me as
essential." And even that duty was not a strongly felt
one: "I think the want of opportunity suspends the force
of duty to receive the Lord's Supper." Wade, op.cit.,
pp. 152, 158, and 172.

107. The Doctrines and Discipline, op.cit., p. 40.

108. Journal of the General Conference of the Methodist Episcopal Church, 1832, I, p. 394.

109. Gilbert Haven and Thomas Russell, Life of Father
Edward Taylor, the Sailor Preacher, Boston, The Boston
Port and Seaman's Aid Society, 1904, p. 266.

110. For descriptions of black religious dance, see
Lynne Fauley Emery, "Sacred Dance," Black Dance in the
United States from 1619 to 1970, Palo Alto, National
Press Books, 1972, pp. 119-138. There has been a pro-
liferation of volumes on nineteenth century black spirituals; but a few of the better works are: Bernard Katz,
ed., The Social Implications of Early Negro Music in the
United States, New York, Arno Press and the New York
Times, 1969, especially Katz's "Introduction" at pages
vii-xviii and John Lovell, Jr.'s "The Social Implications
of the Negro Spiritual" at pages 128-137. For more gen-
eral commentaries, see James H. Cone, The Spirituals
and the Blues: An Interpretation, New York, Seabury
Press, 1972; Miles M. Fisher, Negro Slave Songs in the
United States, New York, Russell and Russell, 1968; and
George Pullen Jackson, White and Negro Spirituals, New
York, J. J. Augustin, 1943.

111. Albert J. Raboteau, Slave Religion: The "Invisible Institution" in the Antebellum South, New York,
Oxford University Press, 1978, pp. 134-150.

112. Ibid., p. 217. For a thorough discussion of
these evening meetings, see pp. 214-219.

113. James Hastings Nichols, Corporate Worship in
the Reformed Tradition, Philadelphia, Westminster Press,
1968, p. 148.

114. At the end of some camp meetings, there would
be separate communion services held around the encamp-
ment where each different denomination would draw together its own members; but the communion was not a common one at the center of the camp worship services. Cf.
Charles Johnson, The Frontier Camp Meeting, Dallas,
Southern Methodist University Press, 1955.

115. Samuel Rogers, Toils and Struggles of the Olden
Times, ed. John I. Rogers, Cincinnati, Standard Publishing Company, 1880, p. 29. Such passing of the peace was
also a feature of Sandemann's churches.

116. Robert Richardson, Memoirs of Alexander Campbell,
1868, II, pp. 129 and 411.

117. Ibid., I, p. 450.

118. Gates, The Early Relation and Separation of Baptists and Disciples, op.cit., passim.

119. Richardson, Memoirs of Alexander Campbell,
op.cit., II, p. 125.

120. Campbell, The Christian System, op.cit., pp. 351-354.

CHAPTER V

1. Calvin Stowe, "Sketches," The Congregational Quarterly, VI, 3, (July, 1864), p. 224.
2. Haven, Life of Father Taylor, op.cit., p. vii. For discussion on these foci of scholarly and popular sermons of the late eighteenth and early nineteenth centuries, see Adams, Humor in the American Pulpit from George Whitefield through Henry Ward Beecher, op.cit., passim.
3. Raboteau, Slave Religion, op.cit., pp. 239ff.
4. William Ames, The Substance of Christian Religion, or a Plain and Easie Draught of the Christian Catechisme, in LII Lectures, on Chosen Texts of Scripture, for Each Lord's Day of the Year (before 1633), London, printed by T. Mabb for Thomas Davies, 1659.
5. William Perkins, "A Discourse of Conscience" (1596), in Pioneer Works on Casuistry, ed. Thomas Merril, Nieuwkoop, B. deGraaf, 1966.
6. John Cotton, God's Promise to his Plantations, Boston, Samuel Green, 1686 (reprint of the 1634 London edition).
7. Samuel Willard, A Sermon Preached on Ezekiel ... Occasioned by the Death of John Leverett, Governor of Massachusetts, Boston, John Foster, 1679.
8. William Laud, "To King James on the King's Birthday," Works, Oxford, John Henry Parker, 1847, I, 1.
9. Samuel Willard, The Duty of a People that have Renewed their Covenant with God, Boston, John Foster, 1680.
10. Increase Mather, "Birth Sin," Five Sermons on Several Subjects, Boston, B. Green, 1719.
11. Cf. Jonathan Edwards, Sinners in the Hands of an Angry God, Boston, Kneeland and Green, 1741. Jonathan Edwards, Christ the Great Example of Gospel Ministers, Boston, T. Fleet, 1750. Samuel Hopkins, The Importance and Necessity of Christians Considering Jesus Christ in the Extent of His High and Glorious Character, Boston, Kneeland and Adams, 1768. Nathanael Emmons, "Rational Preaching," Sermons on Various Subjects of Christian Doctrine and Duty, Providence, John Miller and John Hutchens, 1823, sermon IV. Charles Chauncy, Christian Love Exemplified by the First Christian Church, Boston, Thomas Leverett, 1773.
12. Alden Vaughan, ed., The Puritan Tradition in America, 1620-1730, New York, Harper and Row, 1972, pp. 201 and 203.
13. Elias Keach's arrival in America in 1686 began a period of increased hymn singing among Baptists. Their first compilation of hymns published in America was

entitled <u>The Newport Collection</u>, Philadelphia, Franklin, 1766 and contained 74 hymns for the Lord's Supper.

14. The checklist of Kellogg lithographs to which I contributed during my year as Smithsonian Fellow in art history is to be published by Jacques Schurre in New York.

15. Cf. Doug Adams, "Devils and Disunion: Humor in a Half Century of Popular American Religious Lithographs (1830-1880)," <u>Abstracts, AAA 1975 Annual Meeting</u>, Walter Moore, ed., Council on the Studies of Religion, Waterloo, 1975, pp. 22-23. Examples of American Lithographs with presidents as the devil are "Office Hunters for the Year 1834," (Imbert, 1834); "Polk's Dream," (Baillie, 1946); and "I Adjure All Men to Obey the Behests of King Cotton Under Penalty of Hell Flames," (Meier, 1861). For other portrayals of the devil in American prints, cf. Frank Weitenkampf, <u>Political Caricature in the United States in Separately Published Cartoons, An Annotated List</u>, New York, New York Public Library, 1953, pp. 12, 13, 23, 27, 29, 32, 36, 38, 47, 49, 57, 60, 65, 72, 74, 84, 85, 95, 102, 106, 112, 128, 129, 138, 143, 148, 151, 155, 161; and William Murrell, <u>A History of American Graphic Humor</u>, New York, Whitney Museum of Art, 1933, pp. 20, 31, 37, 41, 45, 47, 62, 75, 101, 102, 109, 124, 129.

16. John Cotton, <u>Exposition on the Thirteenth Chapter of the Revelation</u>, London, 1656, p. 77.

17. Samuel West, <u>A Sermon Preached Before the Honorable Council</u>, Boston, Gill, 1776; reprinted in <u>Religious Origins of the American Revolution</u>, ed. Page Smith, Missoula, Scholars Press, 1976, p. 183.

BIBLIOGRAPHY

Primary Sources

Ainsworth, Henry, Defence of the Holy Scriptures, Worship
    and Ministrie Used in the Christian Churches Separated
    from Antichrist: Against the Challenges, Cavils, and
    Contradiction of Mr. Smythe, in B. Hanbury, Historical
    Memorials Relating to the Independents, I, London, 1839.
Ames, William, The Substance of Christian Religion, or a
    Plain and Easie Draught of the Christian Catechisme, in
    LII Lectures, on Chosen Texts of Scripture, for Each
    Lord's Day of the Year, London, T.Mabb for Davies, 1659.
Andrewes, Lancelot, "On the Third Commandment," Works,
    Oxford, J.H. Parker, 1854, Vol.5, No.2.
_____, "On the Resurrection," Works, Oxford, J.H. Parker,
    1854, Vol.3, No.17.
Ashton, Robert, ed., The Works of John Robinson, I-III,
    Boston, Doctrinal Tract and Book Society, 1851.
Asbury, Francis, The Journal and Letters, I-II, ed., Elmer
    T. Clark, J. Manning Potts, and Jacob S. Payton,
    Nashville, Abingdon Press, 1958.
Beecher, Charles, ed., Autobiography, Correspondence, Etc.,
    of Lyman Beecher, D.D., New York, Harper & Brothers,1865.
Bradford, William, Bradford's History of Plimouth Planta-
    tion, Boston, Wright and Potter, 1901.
Burnyeat, John, "Journal of Life and Gospel Labours of
    John Burnyeat," 1691, in A Selected Series, Biographical
    Narrative, V, ed., John Barclay, London, 1839.
Campbell, Alexander, The Christian System In Reference To
    the Union of Christians and Restoration of Primitive
    Christianity As Plead By The Current Reformation,
    St. Louis, Christian Publishing Company, 1839.
Cartwright, Thomas, "Speech at Contract Making Between His
    Daughter ...," Cartwrightiana, ed., Albert Peel and
    Leland H. Carlson, London, Allen and Unwin, 1951.
Chauncy, Charles, Breaking of Bread in Remembrance of the
    Dying Love of Christ, a Gospel Institution: Five Sermons
    on the Lord's Supper, Boston, 1772.
_____, Christian Love Exemplified by the First Christian
    Church, Boston, Thomas Leverett, 1773.
Clarke, John, Ill Newes From New England: A Narration ...,
    London, 1652.
The Complete Writings of Roger Williams, I-VII, New York,
    Russell and Russell, 1963.
Congregational Order: The Ancient Platforms of the Congre-
    gational Churches of New England, Hartford, Hunt, 1845.
Cotton, John, Christ the Fountaine of Life, London, 1651.
_____, Exposition on the Thirteenth Chapter of the
    Revelation, London, 1656.
_____, God's Promise to his Plantations, Boston, Samuel
    Green, 1686 (reprint of the 1634 London edition).

149

Cotton, John, Letter, John Cotton to R. Levitt, (in re-
sponse to Levitt's inquiry of March 3, 1625) Massachu-
setts Historical Collections, 2nd Series, Volume X.
_____, A Modest and Cleare Answer to Mr. Ball's Discourse
of Set Formes of Prayer, London, 1642.
_____, A Practical Commentary or an Exposition ... Upon
the First Epistle Generall of John, London, 1656.
_____, Singing of Psalms, a Gospel Ordinance, London, 1650.
_____, A Treatise of the Covenant of Grace, London, 1659.
_____, The True Constitution of a Particular Visible
Church Proved by Scripture, London, 1642.
_____, The Way of the Churches of Christ in New England,
London, 1645.
_____, The Way of Congregational Churches Cleared, London,
1648.
Davenport, John, An Answer of the Elders of the Severall
Churches in New-England unto Nine Positions Sent Over
to Them, London, 1643.
The Doctrines and Discipline of the Methodist Episcopal
Church, Philadelphia, Hall for Dickins, 1792.
Dwight, Timothy, Theology Explained and Defended in a
Series of Sermons, I-IV, New York, Harper and Brothers,
1848.
Ecclesiastical Records, State of New York, Albany, James
B. Lyon, 1901-1905, I-VI.
Edwards, Jonathan, Christ the Great Example of Gospel
Ministers, Boston, T. Fleet, 1750.
_____, Sinners in the Hands of an Angry God, Boston, Knee-
land and Green, 1741.
_____, Thoughts on the Revival of Religion in New England,
New York, American Tract Society.
Emerson, Ralph Waldo, ed., The Complete Works of Ralph
Waldo Emerson, XI, Boston and New York, Houghton Mif-
flin Company, 1903-1904.
Emmons, Nathanael, "Rational Preaching," Sermons on Vari-
ous Subjects of Christian Doctrine and Duty, Sermon IV,
Providence, John Miller and John Hutchens, 1823.
Finney, Charles Grandison, Lectures on Revivals of Reli-
gion, William G. McLoughlin, ed., Cambridge, Belknap
Press of Harvard University Press, 1960.
Flint, Timothy, Recollections of the Last Ten Years, Bos-
ton, Cummings, Hilliard, and Company, 1826.
Garrettson, Freeborn, The Experience and Travels of Mr.
Freeborn Garrettson, Philadelphia, Hall, 1791.
Gillette, A.D., ed., Minutes of the Philadelphia Baptist
Association from 1707 to 1807, American Baptist Publica-
tion Society, 1851.
Grabo, Norman S., Edward Taylor's Treatise Concerning the
Lord's Supper, Michigan State University Press, 1966.
Hall, Michael G., ed., "The Autobiography of Increase
Mather," Proceedings of the American Antiquarian Soci-
ety, Worchester, 1962, Vol. 71.
Hooker, Richard, "A Remedy against Sorrow and Fear, deli-
vered in a Funeral Sermon," Works, Seventh Ed., Oxford,
Clarendon Press, 1888, Vol. 13, No. 4.
Hooker, Thomas, Survey of the Summe of Church Discipline,

London, 1648.

Hopkins, Samuel, The Importance and Necessity of Christians Considering Jesus Christ in the Extent of His High and Glorious Character, Boston, Kneeland and Adams, 1768.

Hosmer, James, ed., Winthrop's Journal, I-II, New York, Barnes and Noble, 1953.

Journal of the General Conference of the Methodist Episcopal Church, 1832, I.

Knapp, Jacob, Autobiography of Elder Jacob Knapp, New York, Sheldon and Company, 1868.

Laud, William, "To King James on his Accession," Works, Oxford, John Henry Parker, 1847, Vol. I, No. 2.

_____, "To King James on the King's Birthday," Works, Oxford, John Henry Parker, 1847, Vol. No. 1.

Lechford, Thomas, Plain Dealing or News from New England, London, Johnson Reprint Corporation, 1969.

Lee, Jesse, A Short History of the Methodists in the United States of America, Beginning in 1766, and Continued Till 1809, Baltimore, Magill and Clime, 1810.

The Life and Death of Mr. Henry Jessey, n.p., 1671.

Mather, Cotton, Diary of Cotton Mather, New York, Frederick Ungar Publishing Company.

_____, Magnalia Christi Americana, London, 1702.

_____, Magnalia Christi Americana, Hartford, 1855.

_____, Magnalia Christi Americana, New York, Russell and Russell, 1967.

_____, Magnalia Christi Americana, Cambridge, The Belknap Press of Harvard University Press, 1977.

_____, Ratio Disciplinae Fratrum Nov-Anglorum: A Faithful Account of the Discipline Professed and Practised in the Churches of New-England, Boston, 1726.

Mather, Increase, "Birth Sin," Five Sermons on Several Subjects, Boston, B. Green, 1719.

_____, A Call from Heaven to the Present and Succeeding Generations ..., Boston, 1679.

_____, Discourse Concerning the Danger of Apostasy ..., Boston, 1679.

_____, A Dissertation, Wherein the Strange Doctrine Lately Published in a Sermon, the Tendency of which is to Encourage Unsanctified Persons (while such) to Approach the Holy Table of the LORD, is Examined and Confuted, Boston, 1708.

_____, The Order of the Gospel, Professed and Practiced by the Churches of Christ in New England, Justified, Boston, 1700.

_____, Practical Truths Tending to Promote the Power of Godliness, Boston, 1682.

Mather, Richard, Church-government and Church-covenant Discussed, London, 1643.

McGiffert, Arthur Cushman, Jr., ed., Young Emerson Speaks: Unpublished Discourses on Many Subjects, Boston, Houghton Mifflin Company, 1938.

Mayhew, Jonathan, "Discourse Concerning Unlimited Submission," Sermons, New York, Arno, 1969.

Moody, Dr. Robert, ed., Province and Court Records of

Maine, III, Portland, Maine History Society, 1947.

Morton, Nathaniel, New-Englands Memorial: Or, A Brief Relation of the Most Memorable and Remarkable Passages of the Providence of God, Manifested to the Planters of New-England in America; With Special Reference to the First Colony Thereof, Called New-Plimouth, Cambridge, 1669.

The Newport Collection, Philadelphia, Franklin, 1766.

Nickalls, J.L., ed., The Journal of George Fox, Cambridge, Cambridge University Press, 1952.

Noyes, James, The Temple Measured, London, 1647.

Parker, Thomas, True Copy of a Letter Written by Mr. T.P. ... Declaring his Judgment Touching the Government Practised in the Churches of New England, London, 1644.

Perkins, William, "A Discourse of Conscience," in Pioneer Works on Casuistry, Thomas Merril, ed., Nieuwkoop, B. deGraaf, 1966.

Pierce, Richard D., ed., The Records of the First Church in Boston 1630-1868, Publication of the Colonial Society of Massachusetts, Vol. 39-41, Boston, 1961.

_____, The Records of the First Church in Salem Massachusetts 1629-1736, Salem, Essex Institute, 1974.

Pilmore, Joseph, Journal, Frederick E. Maser and Howard T. Maag, ed., Philadelphia, Message Publishing Co., 1969.

"Plymouth Church Records," Publications of the Colonial Society of Massachusetts, XXII-XXIII, Boston, Colonial Society of Massachusetts, 1920-1923.

Pope, Robert G., ed., The Notebook of the Reverend John Fiske, 1644-1675 (Publications of the Colonial Society of Massachusetts) Boston, 1974, XLVII.

Proceedings of the Bishop and Presiding Elders of the Methodist Episcopal Church in Council Assembled at Baltimore, on the First Day of December, 1789, Baltimore, Goddard and Angell, 1789.

Rathband, William, A Brief Narration of Some Courses, 1694.

Richardson, Robert, Memoirs of Alexander Campbell, II, 1868.

Rogers, Samuel, Toils and Struggles of the Olden Times, John I. Rogers, ed., Cincinnati, Standard Publishing Company, 1880.

Shurtleff, Nathaniel, ed., Records of the Governor and Company of the Massachusetts Bay in New England, IV, Boston, 1853.

Smith, John, Paralleles, Censures, Observations, n.p., 1609.

Sprague, William B., ed., Annals of the American Pulpit, I-IX, New York, Robert Carter and Bros., 1857-1869.

Stimson, H.K., From the Stage Coach to the Pulpit, St. Louis, R.A. Campbell, 1874.

Stoddard, Solomon, An Appeal to the Learned ... Against the Exceptions of Mr. Mather, Boston, 1709.

_____, The Doctrine of Instituted Churches, Explained and Proved from the Word of God, London, 1700.

_____, The Inexcusableness of Neglecting the Worship of God, Boston, 1708.

_____, The Safety of Appearing at the Day of Judgment in the Righteousness of Christ: Opened and Applied, Boston, 1687.

Thomas, M. Halsey, ed., The Diary of Samuel Sewall, I-II,
   New York, Farrar, Straus, and Giroux, 1973.
Tinker, Reuben, Sermons, New York, A. Roman and Co., 1869.
"The Trial of Ezekiel Cheever before the Church at New
   Haven ... 1649," Collections, I, Hartford, Connecticut
   Historical Society, 1860.
Walker, Williston, The Creeds and Platforms of Congrega-
   tionalism, New York, Scribner, 1893.
_____, The Creeds and Platforms of Congregationalism,
   Boston, Pilgrim Press, 1960.
Walter, Thomas, The Ground and Rules of Music Explained
   or an Introduction to the Art of Singing by Note, Fitted
   to the Meanest Capacity, Boston, 1721.
Wesley, John, A Consise Ecclesiastical History, IV, London
   Paramore, 1781.
_____, Letters, J. Telford, ed., London, Epworth Press,
   1931.
West, Samuel, A Sermon Preached Before the Honorable Coun-
   cil, Boston, Gill, 1776; reprinted in Religious Origins
   of the American Revolution, Page Smith, ed., Missoula,
   Scholars Press, 1976.
Whitefield, George, Eighteen Sermons Preached by the Late
   Rev. George Whitefield, Joseph Gurney, ed., Boston, 1820.
_____, Fifteen Sermons Preached on Various Important Sub-
   jects, Glascow, James Duncan and Sons, 1792.
Willard, Samuel, The Duty of a People that have Renewed
   Their Covenant with God, Boston, John Foster, 1680.
_____, A Sermon Preached on Ezekiel ... Occasioned by the
   Death of John Leverett, Governor of Massachusetts, Bos-
   ton, John Foster, 1679.
Winslow, Edward, Hypocrisie Unmasked, London, 1646.

                    SECONDARY SOURCES

Adams, Charles Francis, Three Episodes of Massachusetts
   History, Boston, Houghton Mifflin Company, 1894.
Adams, Doug, "Changing Biblical Imagery and American Iden-
   tity in Seventeenth and Eighteenth Century Sermons and
   Arts," Papers for the Annual Meeting of the American
   Academy of Homiletics, Charles Rice, ed., Atlanta,
   American Academy of Homiletics, 1982.
_____, "Devils and Disunion: Humor in a Half Century of
   Popular American Religious Lithographs (1830-1880),"
   Abstracts, AAA 1975 Annual Meeting, Walter Moore, ed.,
   Council on the Studies of Religion, Waterloo, 1975.
_____, "Free Church Worship in America From 1620 to 1835,"
   Worship (September, 1981) Volume 55, No. 5, pp. 436-440.
_____, Humor in the American Pulpit from George Whitefield
   through Henry Ward Beecher, Austin, The Sharing Co., 1981.
_____, "The Question Period and Authority in Seventeenth
   and Eighteenth Century American Religion," Abstracts of
   AAR and SBL Pacific Northwest Region Annual Meeting:
   May 6-8, 1976, University of Oregon, Eugene, 1976, p.18.
_____, "Religion in Revolution: Bicentennial Perspectives

on Increasing Personal Participation in Worship and the
World: 1776 and 1976," Liturgy, Vol. 20, No. 3 (March,
1975) pp. 72-75.

Baird, Charles W., The Presbyterian Liturgies, Historical
Sketches, Grand Rapids, 1960, Baker Book House.

Baker, Frank, From Wesley to Asbury: Studies in Early
American Methodism, Durham, Duke University Press, 1976.

Baldwin, Alice, The New England Clergy and the American
Revolution, Durham, Duke University Press, 1928.

Barbour, Hugh, The Quakers in Puritan England, New Haven,
Yale University Press, 1964.

Barclay, Robert, The Inner Life of the Religious Societies
of the Commonwealth, London, 1879, third edition.

Bartlett, Robert M. The Faith of the Pilgrims: An American Heritage, New York, United Church Press, 1978.

Beebe, David Lewis, The Seals of the Covenant: The Doc-
trine and Place of the Sacraments and Censures in the
New England Puritan Theology Underlying the Cambridge
Platform of 1648, Th.D. dissertation, Pacific School of
Religion, 1966.

Benes, Peter, ed., New England Meeting House and Church:
1630-1850, Boston, Boston University, 1980.

Bishop, John, "The Methodist Church: A Detailed Survey
of its Worship," Methodist Worship In Relation to Free
Church Worship, Scholars Studies Press, 1975.

Brewer, J. Mason, The Word on the Brazos: Negro Preacher
Tales from the Brazos Bottoms of Texas, Austin, University of Texas Press, 1953.

Brinton, Howard, Friends for 300 Years, New York, Harper
and Row, 1952.

Burrage, Henry, "The Baptist Church in Kittery," Collections of Proceedings of the Maine History Society, Portland, Maine History Society, 1898, Second Series, IX.

Carroll, Kenneth, John Perrot, Early Quaker Schismatic,
London, 1971.

Cooley, Timothy Mather, Sketches of the Life and Character
of the Rev. Lemuel Haynes, A.M., New York, Negro Universities Press, 1969.

Cone, James H., The Spirituals and the Blues: An Interpretation, New York, Seabury Press, 1972.

Curwen, J. Spencer, Studies in Worship Music, London, J.
Curwen and Sons, 1888.

Davies, Horton, Worship and Theology in England from Andrewes to Baxter and Fox, 1603-1690, Princeton, Princeton University Press, 1975.

DeJong, Gerald, The Dutch Reformed Church in the American
Colonies, Grand Rapids, William B. Eerdmans, 1978.

Donnelly, Marian Card, The New England Meeting Houses of
the Seventeenth Century, Middletown, Wesleyan University
Press, 1968.

Earle, Alice Morse, The Sabbath in Puritan New England,
New York, Charles Scribner's Sons, 1896.

Emerson, William, An Historical Sketch of the First Church
of Boston, Boston, 1812.

Emery, Lynne Fauley, "Sacred Dance," Black Dance in the
United States from 1619 to 1970, Palo Alto, National

Press Books, 1972.

Fisher, Miles M., Negro Slave Songs in the United States, New York, Russell and Russell, 1968.

Gates, Errett, The Early Relation and Separation of Baptists and Disciples, Chicago, The Christian Century Company, 1904.

Goen, C.C., Revivalism and Separatism in New England, 1740-1800: Strict Congregationalists and Separate Baptists in the Great Awakening, New Haven and London, Yale University Press, 1962.

Graves, J.R., ed., The First Baptist Church, Memphis, Southern Baptist Book Store, 1890.

Hall, David, ed., The Antinomian Controversy, 1636-1638: A Documentary History, Middletown, Wesleyan University Press, 1968.

_____, The Faithful Shepherd: A History of the New England Ministry in the Seventeenth Century, Chapel Hill, University of North Carolina Press, 1972.

Haven, Gilbert, and Thomas Russell, Life of Father Edward Taylor, the Sailor Preacher, Boston, the Boston Port and Seaman's Aid Society, 1904.

Holifield, E. Brooks, The Covenant Sealed: The Development of Puritan Sacramental Theology in Old and New England, 1570-1720, New Haven, Yale University Press, 1974.

Hubbard, William, History of New England from the Year 1620 to the Year 1680, Boston, Massachusetts Historical Society, 1848.

Jackson, George Pullen, White and Negro Spirituals, New York, J.J. Augustin, 1943.

Jackson, Henry, An Account of the Churches in Rhode Island, Providence, Whitney, 1854.

Johnson, Charles, The Frontier Camp Meeting, Dallas, Southern Methodist University Press, 1955.

Katz, Bernard, ed., The Social Implications of Early Negro Music in the United States, New York, Arno Press and the New York Times, 1969.

King, Henry Melville, The Mother Church: A Brief Account of the Church and Early History of the First Baptist Church in Providence, Philadelphia, American Baptist Publication Society, 1897.

Maxwell, William, A History of Worship in the Church of Scotland, London, Oxford University Press, 1955.

Melton, Julius, Presbyterian Worship in America: Changing Patterns Since 1787, Richmond, John Knox Press, 1967.

Miller, Perry, Orthodoxy in Massachusetts, 1630-1650, A Genetic Study, Cambridge, Harvard University Press, 1933.

_____, and Thomas H. Johnson, ed., The Puritans, New York, Harper and Row, 1963.

Morgan, Edmund, Roger Williams, The Church and the State, New York, Harcourt, Brace and World, 1967.

Murrell, William, A History of American Graphic Humor, New York, Whitney Museum of Art, 1933.

Myers, Albert Cook, Narratives of Early Pennsylvania, West New Jersey, and Delaware, 1630-1707, New York, Barnes and Noble, 1912.

Nichols, James Hastings, Corporate Worship in the Reformed
    Tradition, Philadelphia, Westminster Press, 1968.
Raboteau, Albert J., Slave Religion: The "Invisible In-
    stitution" in the Antebellum South, New York, Oxford
    University Press, 1978.
Scholes, Percy A., The Puritans and Music in England and
    New England, London, Oxford University Press, 1934.
Selleck, George, Quakers in Boston, 1656-1964, Cambridge,
    Friends Meeting at Cambridge, 1976.
Shuffelton, Frank, Thomas Hooker, 1586-1647, Princeton,
    Princeton University Press, 1977.
Solberg, Winton U., Redeem the Time: The Puritan Sabbath
    in Early America, Cambridge, Harvard University Press,
    1977.
Stowe, Calvin, "Sketches," The Congregational Quarterly,
    VI, 3, July, 1864.
Sweet, William Warren, Virginia Methodism, Richmond, Whit-
    tet and Shepperson, 1955.
Tallack, William, George Fox, the Friends, and the Early
    Baptists, London, 1868.
Thomas, Joshua, The American Baptist Heritage in Wales,
    Lafayette, Church History Research and Archives Affili-
    ation, 1976.
Vaughan, Alden, ed., The Puritan Tradition in America,
    1620-1730, New York, Harper and Row, 1972.
Voigt, Edwin E., Methodist Worship in the Church Universal,
    Nashville, Graded Press, 1965.
Wade, William Nash, A History of Public Worship in the
    Methodist Episcopal Church and Methodist Episcopal
    Church, South, from 1789 to 1905, University of Notre
    Dame, Ph.D. dissertation, May, 1981.
Wall, Robert, Massachusetts Bay: The Crucial Decade,
    1640-1650, New Haven, Yale University Press, 1972.
Watkins, Keith, "The Historic Disciple Way," The Breaking
    of Bread: An Approach to Worship for the Christian
    Churches, St. Louis, Bethany Press, 1966.
Wayland, Frances, Notes on the Principles and Practices of
    Baptist Churches, New York, Shelddon, Blakeman, and Com-
    pany, 1857.
White, James F., Protestant Worship and Church Architec-
    ture, New York, Oxford University Press, 1964.
Weitenkampf, Frank, Political Caricature in the United
    States in Separately Published Cartoons, An Annotated
    List, New York, New York Public Library, 1953.
Winslow, Ola, Meetinghouse Hill: 1630-1783, New York,
    Macmillan Company, 1952.
Wood, Nathan, The History of the First Baptist Church of
    Boston, Philadelphia, American Baptist Publication So-
    ciety, 1899.
Ziff, Larzer, The Career of John Cotton: Puritanism and
    the American Experience, Princeton, Princeton University
    Press, 1962.

INDEX

DATE DUE

HIGHSMITH #LO-45220